Other McGraw-Hill Communications Books of Interest

PCS Network Deployment

John Tsakalakis, B.Sc.(Eng.), M.Sc., A.M.I.E.E.

McGraw-Hill
New York   San Francisco   Washington, D.C.   Auckland   Bogotá
Caracas   Lisbon   London   Madrid   Mexico City   Milan
Montreal   New Delhi   San Juan   Singapore
Sydney   Tokyo   Toronto

Library of Congress Cataloging-in-Publication Data

Tsakalakis, John
    PCS network deployment / John Tsakalakis.
       p.   cm.
    Includes index.
    ISBN 0-07-065342-9 (hc)
    1. Personal communication service systems. I. Title.
    TK5103.485.T73   1996
    384.5—dc21   96-47049
                                     CIP

McGraw-Hill

A Division of The McGraw-Hill Companies

1 2 3 4 5 6 7 8 9 0 DOC/DOC 9 0 1 0 9 8 7 6

ISBN 0-07-065342-9

The sponsoring editor for this book was Stephen S. Chapman, the editing supervisor was Paul R. Sobel, and the production supervisor was Donald F. Schmidt. It was set in Arial by Sandra Jamison.

Printed and bound by R. R. Donnelley & Sons Company.

McGraw-Hill books are available at special quantity discounts to use as premiums and sales promotions, or for use in corporate training programs. For more information, please write to the Director of Special Sales, McGraw-Hill, 11 West 19th Street, New York, NY 10011. Or contact your local bookstore.

This book is printed on recycled, acid-free paper containing a minimum of 50% recycled de-inked fiber.

97- 6181
35714849

Contents

Acknowledgments

I would like to thank all colleagues and friends for their support given to me during the preparation of this manuscript.

I would especially like to thank my wife Sandra, for typesetting the manuscript.

This is the first edition and it has taken many late nights and numerous revisions to complete.

The challenge of this industry is to keep up-to-date with all new developments. It is not untypical to report on a topic only to find out that the parameters have changed one month later.

John Tsakalakis

1

Introduction

This book has been written as the result of the author's personal experiences, during the process of designing and planning wireless and wireline networks. The book targets all telecommunication professionals, whether technical or marketing. Hopefully it will give them an insight into the different parameters that have to be considered before and during the design and implementation of a PCS wireless network.

The book covers the fundamentals of switching systems, radio frequency (RF) design parameters, as well as all the main support components involved in a network, specifically Operational Support Systems (OSS), Enhanced Services Platforms (ESP), Billing Systems and Customer Care, as well as Network Management.

Also, this book covers the fundamental required in the set-up of the switching and radio infrastructure, real estate, marketing and economic factors that effect the design and implementation of a PCS network.

Furthermore, the planning process and regulatory environments are explored as well as the different types of emerging radio technologies such as CDMA, TDMA, and GSM among others.

This book should be an invaluable guide to all professionals involved in the wireless industry, whether in the process of designing a wireless network or just having a technical guide they can refer to.

Background

Most operators today have or are in the process of spending hundreds of millions of dollars in the network infrastructure. Most of the expenditure goes to the switching and RF gear. The RF technologies that most of the PCS operators have chosen to go with are summarized in mainly three categories. CDMA, GSM and TDMA (IS136). All these RF technologies will be discussed with more detail in later sections but in practice they all provide an efficient use of the available spectrum by packing more subscribers per frequency block than any previous technologies. All the progress and advances that have been made in the RF transmission area need to also be complemented with as efficient back office systems.

By back office systems I mean, billing systems and customer care, operational support systems, enhanced services, data mediation devices and of course network management systems.

An efficient wireless operation requires state of the art products which consist of discreet network elements adaptable to today's d/emanding environment. These elements will be described more fully in later sections, but the major requirement is the ability to provide support for existing and emerging technologies, as well as provide sufficient operational measurements (OMs) for statistical and operational control.

The typical architectural layout in a wireless environment is typically represented by the following schematic.

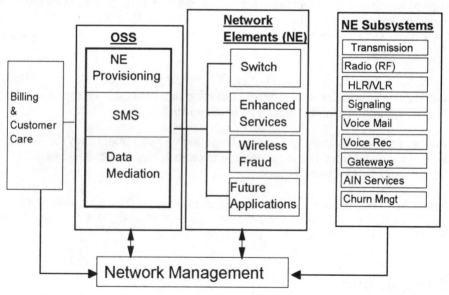

Figure 1:   Back Office Systems Schematic

Network Elements (NEs)

The main elements of a wireless operation in terms of back office systems are as follows:

1.   Switching
2.   Operational Support Systems (OSS)
3.   Enhanced Services
4.   Billing and Customer Care
5.   Network Management
6.   Optional Applications

Switching

This is part of the Network Elements (NEs) which in turn activates the data path that gets transmitted to the subscriber via the RF network. At the handset level the digital signal is converted into analog via a digital to analog converter. Throughout the transmission the signal always remains digital until it reaches the handset. This way privacy as well as data integrity is guaranteed.

The switch is also connected to a Home Location Register which contains information on the location and profile of subscribers and, the Visitors Location Register (VLR) which contains information on the visiting roaming subscribers.

Also, the switch is connected via the signaling system 7 to other switches, networks and services which support advanced signaling techniques.

Transmission, HLR/VLR, RF, and signaling are some of the Network Element (NE) subsystems.

Enhanced Services

This is a robust industrial grade platform designed to run in wireless and wireline applications. It runs on the RS6000 hardware architecture supporting both GSM and AIN based networks. The platform is scalable and expandable to address current customer needs and it supports voice recognition with fully redundant configurations.

Enhanced services is an essential part of the modern infrastructure providing services such as voice mail, voice recognition, gateways to faxes, pagers and other services.

Enhanced services also provide additional services such as text to speech and speech to text conversion as part of the voice recognition support, meet me services, voice dialing, 1800 access, debit card information, multimedia support and others.

Enhanced Services is part of the Network Elements.

Operational Support Systems (OSS)

This is not a Network Element but an intelligent gateway between the upstream systems such as the Billing Systems and the Network Elements. The OSS performs three distinct functions.

- Network Provisioning
- Subscriber Provisioning
- Data Mediation

The OSS interfaces directly to all NEs as well as the Billing System. The Data Mediation part of the OSS allows for the reconstruction and consolidation of partially built up CDR (Call Detail Records) which come from the NEs towards the billing system. Some OSS vendors may not supply the data mediation component. This may have to be purchased separately from other specialized vendors.

The Subscriber Provisioning part allows for the provisioning of new and existing subscribers in a real time fashion and once completed passes all the required instructions to the Network Provisioning module for service activation.

Billing and Customer Care

This is the heart of the upstream system and it absolutely essential that it provides accurate billing with support for flexible rating plans and keeps a record of all accounting information for subsequent billing. The billing can be provided in multiple languages and supports information on roaming subscribers.

Network Management

Voice oriented services are being augmented with data and multimedia services; low speed networks with highspeed ones; closed architecture with open standards; closed access with customer access; equipment specific with integrated systems.

Network Management has two functions. One function is to provide statistical reports related to the performance and capacity of the system, the second function is a maintenance function which alerts the operator of potential faults on specific elements of the network.

The Network Management System uses Operational measurements which are inherent within the NEs and provides an accurate status of the network in Realtime.

More details of of the above Network Elements (NEs) will be described at later sections.

2

System & Technology Introduction

The demand for wireless services and equipment is projected to accelerate rapidly, with worldwide total mobile communications service and equipment revenues growing approximately 20 percent annually during the next five years. This is three times the rate of revenue growth for traditional wire-line communications.

The ability to screen and manage incoming calls will be very important in this new network, as users will only pay for calls they want to accept. Systems will need preference and exception lists and disparate systems will need to communicate with each other more tightly than has been possible so far.

In addition, voice mail systems must communicate with email systems and voice dialers and directory services will also need to communicate between messaging and automated dialing applications. This level of integration demands open standards to fill today's market with applications quickly and also create new markets and applications.

The advent of PCS offers a unique opportunity for service providers to work from a clean slate to build a brand new wireless network. The main challenge will be to select and implement the correct set of value-added services for their customers.

The new network must integrate all these services and provide the bandwidth to support the increased information flow. Service providers must select an open, standards-based platform to ensure they are leveraging available technologies as well as securing a technology platform that can evolve for future growth.

Seven technologies have been standardized for PCS in the United States which can be categorized as follows:

- 4 TDMA based (2 high tier and 2 low tier)
- 3 CDMA based proposal (all high tier)

Cellular 800 MHz			PCS (or CT*) 2 GHz		
Analog	Digital (pre-1995)	Digital (post 1995)	Analog	Digital (pre-1995)	Digital (post 1995)
FDMA AMPS NAMPS TACS SAMTS NMT			NAMPS	CT2* CT2PLUS*	
TDMA	IS-54 GSM E-TDMA	IS-136		CT3* DCS1800	IS-136 based PCS1900 PACS PWT
CDMA					IS-95 based W-CDMA PCS2000

Figure 2: RF History

* In the 900 MHz frequency range

Where,

W-CDMA	= Wideband CDMA
AMPS	= Advanced Mobile Phone Service
CDMA	= Code Division Multiple Access
CT	= Cordless Telephone
DCS 1800	= Digital Cellular System (operating in the 1800 MHz range)
DECT	= Digital European Cordless Telecommunications
E - TDMA	= Extended TDMA
FDMA	= Frequency Division Multiple Access
PWT	= Personal Wireless Telecommunications (based on DECT)
GSM	= Global System for Mobile Communications
NAMPS	= Narrowband AMPS
NMT	= Nordic Mobile Telephone
PCS2000	= Composite CDMA/TDMA/FDMA used by Omnipoint Corp.
SAMTS	= South African Mobile Telephone Service
TACS	= Total Access Cellular System
TDMA	= Time Division Multiple Access
PACS	= Personal Access to Communication Systems
IS	= Interim Standard

Cellular

A decade ago, there were less than 100,000 cellular telephone users in the USA. Now, with over six million new subscribers between June 1993 and June 1994, the cellular industry is growing at a record-breaking pace.

These new users represent an increase of approximately 48 percent since mid-year 1993, bringing cellular subscriber levels to over 31 million by the end of 1995. Cellular availability covers approximately 52 percent of the continental United States and approximately 95 percent of the United States population.

Cellular revenues have exploded from $175 million in 1984 to almost $11 billion in 1993 and are projected to reach $100 billion by the year 2000.

Cellular telephone prices have decreased substantially in the last several years and cellular providers often use phones as a loss leader to entice subscribers to order cellular services.   Cellular service prices are also dropping steadily, but not as rapidly as phone prices.   This demand for services represents a tremendous revenue stream to cellular providers and a unique opportunity to services platform and solutions providers.

The following table indicates the number of cellular subscribers in the top 7 countries in the world. The figures are based on mid-1995 statistics as quoted in the April 1996 issue of the Cellular Business Magazine.

	Country	Subscriber
1	USA	31,000,000
2	Japan	5,347,100
3	United Kingdom	4,449,316
4	Germany	2,932,757
5	Italy	2,862,597
6	China	2,501,193
7	Australia	2,351,000

Figure 3: Cellular Subscribers

Paging

For many users, paging service is an attractive alternative to cellular service. Paging service coverage is highly scaleable. It can be very broad (nationwide) or very narrow (metropolitan area), and can therefore be a very cost-effective mobile messaging solution. The pager itself can be numeric or alphanumeric. It is portable and unobtrusive, requiring very little power.

Paging technology continues to evolve, with two-way paging capabilities and services being introduced. Site paging, the ability to reach a party within an office or campus environment, is also fueling much of the interest and growth in this market. Service costs can range from $10 to $100 per month depending on the pager and services selected.

The number of subscribers to paging services in countries around the world is expected to increase sharply during this decade. One industry report projects aggregate world paging subscribers to increase from 44 million in 1993 to more than 130 million by 1999.

With almost 20 million pagers in service by 1993, the United States currently has the largest, most dynamic paging market in the world. North American paging service revenues were approximately $3.25 billion in 1994.

This market is estimated to grow to over 40 million pagers in service by 1999, or 15 percent market penetration. One exciting growth area will be two-way messaging services offered through the new PCS frequencies.

Specialized Mobile Radio (SMR)

SMR networks provide wireless communication services to closed user groups, such as taxi, delivery, and trucking companies. During the last few years, SMR carriers have expanded their services from basic voice communications to include paging and data communications.

Often referred to as Enhanced Specialized Mobile Radio (ESMR), these services use the latest technologies such as digital cellular. SMR providers operate in the 800 MHz and 900 MHz bands, and since they are not considered common carriers, their rates are not regulated.

Through FCC regulations and alliances with common carriers, these private radio networks may soon be able to connect with public switched telephone and cellular networks, competing directly with cellular service providers and equipment manufacturers.

SMR offers broad, established coverage and is a cost-effective alternative to cellular. There were almost 2 million SMR subscribers by 1993. The total SMR equipment market is estimated to increase from $760 million in 1993 to $1.24 billion in 1996.

Nextel is the largest SMR provider in the United States. Nextel recently formed an alliance with Motorola to turn its older radio technology into a sophisticated cellular network. In Canada, Clearnet is offering similar SMR services, as well as having won one of the newly awarded PCS licenses.

PCS

The FCC has defined PCS as "a family of mobile or portable radio communications services which could provide services to individuals and businesses, and be integrated with a variety of competing networks."

PCS is envisioned to provide the next generation of wide-area, high-mobility services which compete with the rapidly growing cellular service, and innovations for alternative or complementary local loop services, wireless local area networks (LANs), wireless private branch exchanges (PBXs), and pedestrian two-way communications similar to existing PCTS.

The Personal Communications Industry Association (PCIA) defines telecommunications service as "an integrated set of system features and functions which provides an ability to give or exchange information over a distance," and personal communications service (PCS) as "a broad range of individualized telecommunications services that enable people or devices to communicate independent of location."

The term "PCS" is commonly associated with emerging telecommunications services that are considered to be "personal" and "universal." The personal aspect is the ability of individuals to communicate independent of time, location, technology (e.g., wired or wireless), and type of information (e.g., voice, data, or video) with minimum user input and maximum flexibility.

The universal aspect of PCS has two general meanings. First, "universal" refers to the ability of service providers to provide a wide variety of services to a broad segment of the population. Second, "universal" refers to the ability of service providers to meet end-users' expectations that their terminal devices will be able to access "like" services independent of service provider, geographic location, technology, and time of day.

Recent auctions of PCS frequencies in the United States, privatization of telecommunications in South America, the introduction of local and long distance competition in Europe, and developing telecommunications needs and infrastructure in remote and developing countries are also stimulating the awareness and growth of wireless services.

In the past, there has been only minimal competition among wireless communication services, and virtually no competition between wireless and wire-line telecommunication services. The introduction of PCS will expand the already exploding wireless communications industry and compete with the existing cellular industry.

Long-distance carriers, hoping to reduce the $21 billion they pay each year to the regional Bell companies for access to their local phone networks, are looking to PCS as a way to sidestep such charges. The promise of ubiquitous, feature-rich, low cost communications service will compel cellular providers to respond by lowering prices while offering competitive services and features to potentially new mobile telephony subscribers as well as their installed base.

Summary

The conclusions are irrefutable and the business implications are profound worldwide, all segments of the wireless communications market are experiencing explosive growth. Technology developments and the need to access people and information are fueling the demand for new services to address this people-in-motion market.   Hence, the need for convenient, user-friendly applications will continue to grow as users demand better, faster, and more powerful integrated solutions.

The challenge for integration will be compounded by users on multiple systems requiring close integration of services between applications on both Customer Premise Equipment (CPE) and Public Switched Telephone/Advanced Intelligent Network (AIN) equipment combined with a host of support applications such as Operational Support Systems, Enhanced Services, Integrated Network Management, Billing Systems, Wireless Fraud Applications and others.

There are tremendous revenue opportunities for companies that are poised to address the demand for these enhanced services and applications.

Rapid time to market and the need for equipment and services to inter-operate and tightly integrate will dictate that platforms and solutions be based on open standards and architectures. Companies that base their solutions on Signal Computing Systems Architecture (SCSA) are already delivering leading edge, feature-rich applications tailored for the wireless market.

National Licenses

Worldwide, most nations that have addressed the licensing of PCS and cellular have chosen to license these services on a nationwide basis. The United Kingdom, for example, authorized two cellular and PCN licenses -- all nationwide. Germany issued two nationwide digital cellular licenses -- one to DBT Telecom, the other to Mannesmann Mobilfunk GmbH. Germany has also announced its intention to award a third nationwide license in the 1800 MHz band.

In November 1990, Australia decided to grant three nationwide cellular licenses. AUSTEL, the Australian regulatory agency, studied the possible structure for the third cellular license and reported its findings July 31, 1991.

In that study AUSTEL explicitly considered whether to grant regional or nationwide licenses when considering opening up a third cellular band. AUSTEL concluded that a third nationwide licensee would enhance domestic and international competitiveness, and would simplify international roaming agreements.

In short, nationwide licenses are the rule internationally, with the United States being one of the few exceptions. The rationale for such licenses, expressed most clearly by AUSTEL, is the superior economic efficiency of such arrangements.

In the United States, the FCC has nearly completed the auctioning of PCS Licenses. A and B Frequency "Blocks" (99 MTA licenses) were auctioned for more than $7 billion, C Block auctions (492 Basic Trading Areas (BTA) 30 MHz licenses) began on December 8, 1995 and concluded in May 1996, providing the most lucrative federal auction reaping $10.2 billion for the U.S. Treasury Department. Blocks D, E and F (492 BTA 10 MHz licenses each) are planned to begin around 3Q96.

In Canada, a decision by Industry Canada to create multiple nationwide PCS licenses had significant precedent, particularly in situations such as this "where such grants would expedite delivery of a new and innovative service to the public."

Such benefits have included better overall satisfaction of the growing consumer demand for the service; expedited service availability flowing from a high degree of technical and equipment standardization; a superior ability to provide enhanced services through such standardization; easier and cheaper frequency and billing coordination; and stimulation of spectrum efficiency by providing incentives for investment, research and development in new technologies.

In Canada, on December 18, 1995 Industry Canada (IC) awarded four PCS licenses to the following companies. MicroCell and Clearnet were awarded a

30 MHz spectrum with immediate opportunity for deployment, and Bell Mobility and Cantel were awarded a spectrum of 10 MHz scheduled for deployment 3 years later. The delay in deploying their PCS network for the two latter companies was based on the premise that since they already own current cellular licenses in the 800 MHz band, it would only be fair to the two newcomers to give them time to catch up.

As shown below, all of these and additional benefits will be realized if nationwide PCS authorizations are issued.

There are a variety of standards that will likely be adopted for PCS in North America, including TDMA, narrowband CDMA, broadband CDMA, and DCS 1900 (the standard for British PCN). One of the most powerful benefits that nationwide licensees can bring to PCS is the early adoption and implementation of a set of technical standards on a nationwide basis.

Early selection of common PCS technical standards serves important policy goals:

- Facilitates the infrastructure needed to support nationwide roaming.
- Makes it easier for manufacturers to develop equipment necessary for PCS by assuming a nationwide equipment market for manufacturers.
- Permits the achievement of economies of scale in the production of network and terminal equipment.
- Promotes rapid investment by service providers and manufacturers alike.
- Promotes the development of new markets.
- Promotes spectrum sharing with incumbent microwave users, as the latter users gain confidence that their links will not be interrupted by non-standard devices.

Conversely, until a set of technical standards is adopted, it is difficult to envision the rapid development of an equipment industry exploiting what appear to be very large potential economies of scale. In view of the highly competitive character of the equipment industry, worldwide, it seems the advantages of an early start in the exploitation of what might well prove to be an exploding market would be very great.

It is not advantageous to specific countries for the regulatory bodies to set technical standards for PCS, given the nearly completed work of the JTC to endorse multiple qualified standards. Therefore, the marketplace is left to set standards for PCS; the issue becomes which geographic licensing scheme best facilitates this process. In this regard, nationwide licenses offer significant advantages.

First, nationwide licensees will have the resources and powerful incentives to settle upon a set of standards, and the ability to implement such standards promptly. They will also constitute a market or separate markets each large enough to induce equipment manufacturers to design and supply necessary equipment.

In addition, nationwide licensees will have the incentives to choose the best PCS standards, because they will bear the costs if their standard choices turn out badly; if competitors make a better choice of technology, for example, nationwide licensees will calculate the respective costs of remaining with their original choices or of abandoning them and moving to new technology.

As suggested above, the ability of nationwide licensees to adopt PCS technical standards on an expedited basis will speed dramatically the construction of a nationwide PCS network. Nationwide licensees will also provide management with the legal control to design and construct a nationwide PCN in the most efficient configuration to serve the largest number of consumers. Such management and design efficiencies will speed the rollout of a PCS system that will likely serve a great number of people more cheaply than cobbling together a national network of local or regional licensees after the fact.

In addition, the capital requirements for a nationwide PCS build will be a substantial one. A nationwide license, with its economies of scale and scope and elimination of the transaction costs of amalgamating smaller systems, will be much more attractive in terms of obtaining capital financing by providing tremendous investment incentives and reducing investment risk. Costs of financing should be lower in percentage terms.

Further, large PCS service areas will reduce the costs of interference coordination between PCS licensees; a nationwide licensee offers the greatest opportunity for efficient channel management. Increases in the geographic extent of an operator's service territory lead to efficiency increases in the operator's frequency reuse plan. This is because an operator that can extend its service territory into adjacent markets will reduce the need for frequency coordination at the boundaries of neighboring systems.

If Operator A negotiates and acquires Operator B, the boundary between the two systems effectively disappears, and A can now manage its channel use over a larger area without the need to coordinate with B. To the extent that Operator A is able to expand and reduce frequency coordination with adjacent systems, it can more efficiently plan its channel management to match customer demand. Correspondingly, the greatest opportunity for efficient channel management, then, is a nationwide license, which completely eliminates the need for in-band frequency coordination.

Although a scheme of fragmented regions might ultimately achieve similar efficiencies, the expansion of Operator A's territory in the above example obviously incurs increasingly significant transaction costs as the number of geographically separate PCS service territories increases.

Moreover, although interference coordination across system boundaries has not been a major problem in cellular, the problem could be much more significant in PCS, given the lack of a regulatory imposed technical standard (as AMPS was imposed in cellular), the wide range of possible technologies, and market uncertainty.

United States FCC C- Block Winners

In May 1996, the most lucrative federal auction closed, reaping $10.2 billion for the Treasury and setting the stage for unprecedented competition in the U.S. marketplace for wireless communications.

The major winners of the C-Block band are as follows:

- NextWave Personal Communications Inc. has paid $4.2 billion for PCS licenses in 56 markets including New York and Los Angeles.
- DCR Communications Inc. has paid $1.4 billion for 43 markets.
- GWI PCS Inc. has paid $1.1 billion for 14 licenses including one for Atlanta.
- BDPCS Inc. with 17 licenses at $870 million.

Introduction to PCS Deployment and Economics

The cost of obtaining spectrum is only the beginning in calculating the overall economics of PCS deployment. Potential PCS operators also need to consider the costs of site acquisition, infrastructure development and network operations as well as the expense of marketing to customers against well-entrenched cellular carriers and other PCS operators in the same market.

Like any new telecommunications service, these issues are affected by a variety of factors, the impact of which will require careful thought by prospective operators.

The most significant factor is the PCS technology to be deployed, for the flexibility or limitation of the technology determines all other costs of building and operating a PCS system.

As a result, PCS operators will want to choose technologies that require lower capital investment in order to improve the economic potential of their ventures.

Relocation Costs

The spectrum allocated for PCS systems in the 1900 MHz band was system.

As cur previously assigned to operational fixed service (OFS) mixed microwave users, such as oil companies and local police and fire departments. In areas with existing microwave installations, PCS operators will need to relocate these users to other frequency bands.

In addition, some radio technologies will require clearing all of the adjacent spectrum even for initial deployment of a PCS recently written, FCC regulations allow the winners of PCS spectrum to request involuntary relocation of incumbent OFS microwave users after a period of three years and voluntary relocation and arbitration with public-safety users within five years.

However, even if an OFS user were to agree to immediate relocation, it is generally held that this activity will cost approximately $225,000 per link, according to UTAM Inc., the industry manufacturer group recently chartered by the FCC to develop funding and coordinate reallocations of OFS users in the unlicensed PCS bands.

Cell Site Costs

Propagation of the radio signal is substantially lower in the PCS frequency bands (1900 MHz) than in the cellular and Global System for Mobile Communications (GSM) frequency bands (800 900 MHz). This means that for a given area, three to eight times more PCS cells must be installed than would be required with traditional cellular systems.

This requirement dramatically increases the amount of base station equipment to be deployed, the number of sites to be acquired and constructed, and the associated costs of back-hauling traffic between sites for each PCS system.

For example, it has been reported that the recently completed Mercury One-2-One PCS-1800 GSM network in England required more than 500 cell sites at an estimated cost of more than $500 million to cover a 1,900 square-mile area around London.

This equates to 2.5 square miles per cell site, or an average cell radius of under one mile.

While some of these cells were installed to meet capacity demands and provide in-building coverage, most were needed just to provide basic subscriber coverage equivalent to that of cellular service in the United Kingdom. Compare these quantities to the original 800 MHz cellular system covering the entire New York City service area, which required only 24 cell sites for initial coverage.

When planning their systems, PCS operators will need to consider the total number of cells that will be required to provide adequate coverage. The critical variables then become the cost per cell and cost per channel, variables that are different for each proposed PCS technology. While some vendors argue that these cost differences can be overcome by techniques to use spectrum more efficiently, this theory remains unproved.

Antenna, Base Station Costs

Many local governments are not only limiting construction of new towers, but in some areas are seeking to have operators remove existing facilities. Consider what the reaction of local zoning authorities will likely be to permit applications for constructing four to eight times as many towers for each of several PCS operators. In many cases, it may be necessary to negotiate shared sites with other PCS or cellular operators.

Numerous smaller and much less obtrusive cell sites will be a basic environmental condition of any PCS network, regardless of which technology is deployed. Miniaturized base stations (typically less than 10 inches by 10 inches by 18 inches and lighter than 25 pounds) can be easily pole-mounted or attached to the sides of buildings, giving operators greater flexibility in selecting sites and reducing the concerns of local zoning officials.

Proposed PCS Technologies

While a single standard technology will be beneficial in terms of user roaming, reduced costs of building the PCS infrastructure and reduced costs of user equipment from volume production, it is likely that two or three technologies will become de facto standards as they are deployed by PCS operators.

The PCS technology developed by Colorado Springs, Colo.-based Omnipoint Corp. provides for full vehicular mobility and full-coverage PCS. Moreover, Omnipoint's technology allows a single handset and common air interface (CAI) to be used in all three segments of the wireless market public, private business and residential in the licensed or unlicensed PCS or Industrial, Scientific, and Medical (ISM) bands.

Omnipoint's approach makes use of the major advantages of Code Division Multiple Access (CDMA), Time Division Multiple Access (TDMA), and Frequency Division Multiple Access (FDMA) in a hybrid solution. The Omnipoint standard technology (PCS2000) was expected to be available in early 1996.

GSM is the European digital cellular standard, operating at 1800 MHz for PCS services. A modified version of GSM for PCS operation is already available.

Vendors supporting this standard include L.M. Ericsson, Motorola Inc., Nortel, and Nokia Corp.

In North America, the existing TDMA and CDMA cellular technologies have been proposed for "upbanding" to the PCS frequencies. TDMA and CDMA are digital technologies designed for 800 MHz cellular service, but vendors have proposed modified versions that will operate the 1900 MHz bands for PCS.

TDMA uses narrowband channels, separating multiple calls within the channels, separating multiple calls within the channel by assigning them to a separate time slot. The modified version of TDMA technology is expected to be available to PCS operators in early 1996.

However, narrowband TDMA-only systems do not provide any means for interference rejection nor can they guarantee the system will not create substantial interference to OFS microwave users. This interference potential multiplies by the number of users within a cell, increasing the ramifications for sites with the large number of PCS users.

In TDMA-only systems, frequency sharing with OFS microwave users will be limited solely to avoidance techniques, which may not be acceptable in many geographic areas. This standard is supported AT&T Corp. and Ericsson.

CDMA uses wideband channels, separating multiple calls within the channel by special encoding on each transmission bit. The cost per channel of CDMA-only systems rises linearly with increases in capacity. In addition, CDMA-only systems are highly susceptible to interference, which substantially curtails an operator's ability to reuse channels in a high-density environment such as an office or apartment building.

The modified version of CDMA technology is expected to be available for adoption by PCS operators by mid-1996. CDMA was initially developed for the cellular market by Qualcomm Inc., and the upbanded CDMA standard is supported for PCS by AT&T, Motorola, and Nortel.

Any solution based on "upbanding" a technology that was designed for the entirely different needs of an 800 MHz cellular market will have difficulty succeeding in the multi-operator, highly competitive world of PCS. This is especially true in those areas outside of the larger markets because these networks will have the same cost structure as cellular, but because they require many more cells, all costs of cell deployment and network operation will be substantially higher.

Economic Factors of PCS Site Acquisition

An initial task in PCS deployment is to find appropriate sites for cells and base stations, then negotiate purchase of lease, rights of way, zoning and building permits. Because a large number of sites are required to provide full PCS coverage, it will be challenging to find all the sites while also meeting considerations of cost, zoning and network engineering.

System Infrastructure

Building the PCS network infrastructure is the next task. In a typical PCS system, the radio access portion will account for 75 to 85 percent of the total system cost.

Only 15 to 25 percent of infrastructure costs are attributable to the network switching, operations and related data management systems such as subscriber registers.

PCS operators will want to choose a radio access technology that can be deployed at a lower cost than other mobile RF technologies. This cost differential can translate into savings of hundreds of millions of dollars for a single licensed area and savings of several billion dollars for national coverage.

Traffic Backhaul and Delivery

The costs of interconnecting cell sites must be calculated for all possible installation methods across the entire coverage area. The PCS technology should support interconnection through a variety of media, including low-cost unshielded twisted pair, ISDN Basic Rate Interfaces (BRIs), ISDN Primary Rate Interfaces (PRIs), television coaxial cable, T1 lines (ESF or D4 Framing), and even standard analog voice lines. This support will allow a PCS operator to choose the backhaul method best suited to each application.

In general, PCS technologies that can employ multiple DSOs and fractional T1 circuits offer greater flexibility and lower costs for interconnecting cell sites.

Marketing Costs

Launching a new PCS service will involve enormous costs for marketing to potential customers. Many PCS operators will need to follow the strategy of cellular operators, which have subsidized the cost of handsets in order to gain customers. While this may mean an initial loss, the operators expect the payback to come from usage charges.

Network Operations

PCS operators will want the ability to use existing carrier networks for backbone transport, whether these networks are based on GSM or Advanced Intelligent Network (AIN) standards. This will allow the PCS operators to take advantage of the capacity in these networks (millions of lines), lower costs compared to maintaining their own backbones and greater availability and stability.

Economic Analysis

PCS operators will find it challenging to develop viable business cases for small cities, those outside of the top 20 markets. As described earlier, certain PCS technologies will be difficult to cost-justify in even the largest cities. For smaller cities, this will be even more difficult because of the smaller subscriber base for amortizing network costs.

To illustrate, Colorado Springs is the 109th largest MSA (Metropolitan Statistical Area) in the United States with a population of about 400,000 people. This means that nearly 85 percent of the MSA/RSAs (Rural Service Areas) are smaller than Colorado Springs.

By making the right choice of equipment, a PCS operator could initially deploy a fully mobile system for under $1 million for all radio access (by way of comparison, typically less than the cost of a single McDonald's franchise). This allows the PCS operator to justify and obtain financing since the system will generate positive cash flow after only a small penetration of the local population.

Differentiating Factors

Lower Cost

At a minimum, PCS must be able to deliver coverage that is perceived to be similar to cellular, including in-vehicle use with high-speed handoff. For long-term market differentiation, the PCS operator should be prepared to offer prices that are substantially less than current cellular charges and provide significant new features.

Current cellular technologies (including IS-54, IS-95, and DCS-1900 digital systems) are prone to high infrastructure costs that grow linearly with the growth in subscribers. This keeps the cost of airtime high, making it difficult to economically pursue new markets such as wireless local loop or in-building service.

In addition, the costs of conventional cellular systems increase linearly as the number of subscribers increases. Likewise, PCS systems that are based on 20 to 30 cities.

Instead, a PCS system should be able to optimize price and performance based on the costs of components and other deployment activities. This approach enables wide scale deployment of PCS even in less populated areas.

Wireline Quality

PCS subscribers will expect voice quality that is comparable to wireline services. The PCS technology must support this high quality not only for voice, but also for data.

Traditional cellular cannot provide equivalent-quality, transparent support for data applications, even with such technologies as Cellular Digital Packet Data (CDPD). With PCS, data capabilities will be built into the technology design, including high-speed data and transparent support for standard fax-and-data modems.

Public/Private Operation

Some PCS technologies are designed to allow a single handset and common air interface to operate in both public systems and in private applications (e.g., wireless PBX) using either licensed or unlicensed radio spectrum.

This capability will allow PCS to provide additional value and differentiation when competing against in-building cellular systems such as Southwestern Bell's Freedom Link.

Advanced Feature and Services

PCS technologies should support user features such as personal phone number, caller identification, call screening, and integration of call and paging services in short, any user feature that is or will be supported by existing cellular services, PBXs, or AIN-based central offices.

In addition, the PCS system should interface with existing public network infrastructures to take advantage of the immense experience and existing manufacturing volume behind these technologies.

Making the Right Choice

The economics of PCS deployment encompass a number of variables and their associated costs that require careful consideration for each system.
Beyond the initial expense of acquiring spectrum, the costs of cell site acquisition, equipment purchase and installation, ongoing network operation and marketing services to customers can mount quickly.

All of these costs are impacted by the choice of PCS technology and its ability not only to make efficient use of the spectrum, but of existing network infrastructure and services. By choosing the right PCS technology, an operator can quickly reap the financial rewards of systems deployed in cities large or small.

Timelines

The timelines related to the infrastructure build-up are illustrated in figure 4 . The timelines are for a period of one (1) year which is considered as the minimum possible time to build the basic infrastructure with minimum deployment.

The areas of coverage described in this timeline of the build-up are as follows:

- Switching.
- Real Estate.
- Transmission.
- IT.
- Enhanced Services.
- Back Office systems (e.g. Billing and Customer Care).

It is assumed that the real estate requirements will consist of 9 months spent on site aquisition and the final 3 months on construction of those sites. In switching infrastructure it is assumed that 3 months will be spent on vendor selection then an addition 6 months in the installation of the switching locations alpha and beta testing. The final 3 months will be spent in trial period with "friendly customers".

Transmission requirements and vendor selection will also take 3 months to complete then there will be a delay until the telephone company has installed all the transmission lines (assumed to be between 1 and 2 months). Construction and testing of transmission lines will commence and will be completed by month 11 (eleven). There will be an overlapping period between testing of "friendly customers" and the completion of all transmission lines.

Billing and customer care will take an average of 4 months to define and present the requirements. Thereafter the design, beta testing and verification will follow on before the trial with "friendly customers" commences.
Enhanced services requirements definition will commence about a month after

the switching infrastructure vendor selection has commenced and will also follow the process of requirements definition, implementation, beta testing, verification and "friendly customers" trial.

All above elements have a final stage which is the acceptance by the operator stage.

The figure below represents the above stages:

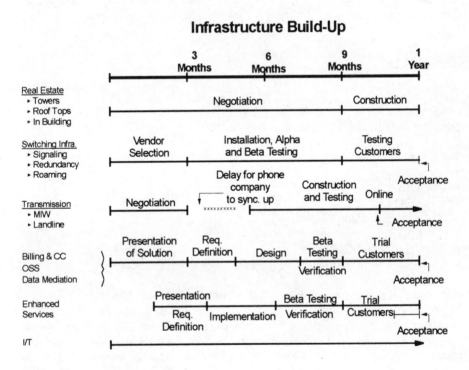

Figure 4: Infrastructure Build-up

3

Introduction to Radio Infrastructure Design

The two current PCS access technologies of choice involve the use of TDMA (time division multiple access, e.g., IS-136, GSM or its derivatives), or CDMA techniques (code division multiple access, e.g., IS-95 CDMA).

GSM (PCS1900)

GSM, Global System for Mobile Communications, utilizes a 200 kHz channel divided into eight time slots with FDD (frequency division duplexing at 80 MHz; with a half rate vocoder it is possible to access 16 time slots). The mobile's receiver and transmitter operate on different frequencies and time slots, and as such do not require duplexed.

Base stations, on the other hand, do require expensive filters for simultaneous transmissions, and the main cost in GSM development is due to such software and computer aided hardware for operation.

GSM, or TDMA in general, requires accurate synchronization of mobile transmissions so that there is adequate separation between channels in use regardless of the distance from the base station. In fact, because of the possibility of multipath delays exceeding the duration of one bit, the receiver must use an equalizer and reacquire synchronization on each slotted transmission burst.

The GSM coding scheme uses a dedicated control channel for registration, locating and setup, a broadcast channel for base station identity and information, and other channels may be used for paging and messaging.

GSM using a 13 kbps voice coder introduces noticeable quantization distortion and causes the need for echo cancellers due to the processing time it requires.

There is the possibility that an enhanced mode vocoder (15.2 kbps) will emerge in late 1996.

GSM is a very demanding system in terms of digital processing resulting in large power drains to the portable with a resulting decrease in battery life due to high levels of RF power emitted from these devices. GSM has high development costs associated with it, but relatively low recurring costs for the equipment. GSM utilizes base station controllers to manage the base stations, all connected to a mobile switching center.

While GSM uses CCITT SS7, it is not fully compatible with US SS7 required for AIN (advanced intelligent networks). The authentication system used is highly secure, using a personalized chips, or smart cards (SIM (subscriber identity module) cards) in conjunction with complex algorithms generated in the various location registers. Use of the transferable smart cards afford users great flexibility in roaming to any other network where GSM technology is deployed.

Diversity Techniques introduced such as coding and interleaving (time diversity), frequency hopping (frequency diversity), the simultaneous use of multiple antennas (spatial diversity) and the use of equalizers (multipath diversity) can be used to enhance the range limits of the GSM system.

Capacity limits can be enhanced through the use of half rate speech coders, discontinuous transmissions, power control, adaptive multi-beam antennas and frequency hopping over the system bandwidth.

CDMA (IS-95)

CDMA (code division multiple access) uses spread spectrum techniques, assigning a unique code to each used connected to the system. The transmit bandwidth used is far greater than the bandwidth required for the information being sent. (IS-95 uses a 1.2288 MHz signal for a 9.6 kbps digital signal for a so-called processing gain of 128).

Since channel capacity is dictated by bandwidth as well as the amount of interference present, a great number of users can be accommodated over a single channel. In fact, the amount of noise that can be tolerated increases logarithmically with increased bandwidth, such that a signal can be sent and received with lower average power than that of the ambient noise level.

CDMA transmits data as PN (pseudo-noise) sequences that, although appearing like random noise, are actually periodic sequences, with the benefit that in general, potential interference is reduced by an amount equal to the processing gain.

The use of forward and reverse power control is critical to the proper operation of CDMA in that, from the controller standpoint, one signal will not mask another. Higher capacity is achieved by keeping all noise levels to an absolute minimum.

Since all signals should arrive at the base station with the same strength, however, implementation of a hierarchical cells (e.g., microcells) operating at different power levels could prove difficult. CDMA uses a variable rate voice coder that reduces its frequency of operation when voice activity is low, effectively increasing capacity levels by up to four times. Note, however, that with higher data rates and a greater number of calls in progress, the size of a CDMA cell effectively becomes reduced.

By orthogonally coding each signal using Walsh functions, perfect isolation between the different signals is achieved. Handoffs from one base station to another are "soft" in that multiple base stations monitor the signal, which remains at the same frequency, with the effect that the handover is transparent to the user with a very low probability of dropped calls.

Of course, this means that the system is always in a high degree of handoffs with an associated high signaling load on the system. In essence, CDMA is excellent in its frequency reuse, capacity and cell size features, although commercially it is a relatively newly emerging technology.

CDMA claims to have a higher capacity, wider range and softer hand off than TDMA (Time Division Multiple Access) based on a small number of trial that have taken place. Effectively this translates to a lower cost infrastructure than TDMA.

RF Planning Tools

In order to optimize the design of a network, it is necessary to use a sophisticated and accurate hardware/software wireless engineering platform. This would require up to date terrain, and demographic and morphological files in the database for determining the best locations of proposed cell sites. Field results would be used to calibrate the accuracy of the predictive model before proceeding with final system design.

For example, Comsearch's MCAP (Mobile Communications Analysis Platform) has such capabilities, and includes such features as the ability to allow the user to vary input parameters such as power and interference levels, bandwidth, vocoder rate probabilities, temperature, morphology, antenna gains and patterns, data rates and call traffic per area. In return, it will yield output on coverage, cell loading service area, path loss, handoffs, best server, ERP levels and link balances.

Propagation Tests

The network design process is an iterative one in that field measurements must be taken to ensure the accuracy of the predictive model before final system design can be relied upon. This can be accomplished best by changing the propagation model used in the prediction software to harmonize with actual results obtained in the field using signal generators and monitoring devices. Resulting contour maps of coverage can then be used for comparative purposes.

Because the output of the predictive software will only be as accurate as the terrain files, it will be necessary to perform visual checks of the areas for verification of any reasons why the model deviates from real world measurements before actually changing the model itself.

Trials

In evaluating any potential technology for its suitability to implementation, it is necessary to perform technical trials. Such trials might include an evaluation of handoff times, and a check as to how the system holds up under various levels of interference and loading before bit error rates (BER) start affecting audio quality.

Tests are performed to determine levels of emissions outside the actual channel being used, the mapping out of signal strengths to determine a cell's range over various terrain characteristics and levels of mobility, and perhaps a mean opinion score (MOS) based on an appraisal by non-technical users.

Of interest also would be to determine how well a system will function inside and outside, ranging anywhere from dense urban to rural environments, determining how much jitter a transmitter could generate that a receiver could tolerate, and the maximum bit rate that could be available by multiplexing sub-channels together (GSM) or by using a higher bit rate with lower processing gain (CDMA).

Planning Process

A commercial design package can be used to determine site placement based initially on convenience of location and expediency. The capacity and range of each of the cells will depend on the actual traffic demand per area, so cell design will then predict coordinates for more sites that will be needed to provide full coverage.

This data will be provided to the appropriate department to negotiate access. If it is found that the requested location is not feasible, the designer will choose another location that appears to provide full coverage until a workable scenario is reached.

In some cases it may be necessary to introduce directional antennas or to sectorize to achieve the desired coverage. In other cases it may be found that an obstruction stands directly in the way of the proposed antenna location that did not appear in the files provided with the database.
This process will obviously require a few iterations to the model until it has been shown that the predicted coverage has in fact been achieved in the real working environment. Then once the facilities are secured, the operator will be assured of full coverage and optimal cell placement.
The model will allow for expansion outward, initially concentrating on the downtown cores of the major cities.

Optimization

Once a system is up and running, it is necessary to further optimize its performance characteristics. Technicians in the field taking measurements will provide raw data that may subsequently reveal coverage gaps (or in some cases an overlap of coverage), ping ponging, dropped calls at certain locales or the fact that system capacity is adversely affected by transmitted emissions outside the operating channel bandwidths and capacity is not found to be as advertised at certain levels of mobility.

At other times, it may be found that the maximum tolerable delay spread has been exceeded, and that certain areas have a higher speech erasure rate than others.

Such factors as dynamic channel allocation or antenna sectorization may have an impact on frequency reuse, or propagation delays may affect propagation diversity strategies.

The introduction of a higher rate vocoder may have an impact on cell capacity as would the application of devices using a net data rate higher than was originally estimated. Again this is an iterative process whereby the network is monitored as it evolves, measurements taken, and changes effected as needed using the latest technological advancements available at the time.

Antennas

In the design process, estimated levels of traffic are the driving force behind determining how many and where cell sites should be located. In some cases it may be necessary to implement sectored cells at the outset. With time, as traffic increases on the system, it will also become apparent that certain cells in the system are becoming overloaded.

This will result in a need to sectorize sites in many cases in order to cope with the demand. In other cases, it may be found desirable to introduce a certain degree of tilt into some of the antenna configurations. Or, keeping in mind that extra transmission components could have an effect on the link budget, the use of remote antennas or distributed antenna arrays may be advised for certain wide areas.

Evolution

As the sophistication of the network increases with time, new technologies and innovations will be introduced as necessary. In conjunction with active participation in forums and industry committees, we will be interested in keeping abreast of developmental work going on in post-secondary institutions and in the private sector.

The development and use of devices such as signal boosters in areas with poor coverage, smart antennas to provide coverage to areas on an as needed basis or antenna arrays to increase trunking efficiency will be of primary interest.

Such devices will need to be appraised and tested in the network to gauge their actual applicability to the field based on performance factors such as how their inception might affect link budgets, how much extra propagation delay can be tolerated and how the system combats increased noise due to the summing of several antenna signals.

4

Introduction to Enhanced Services Platforms (ESP)

This document provides the functional and technical specifications of the Enhanced Services Platform (ESP) that has been designed for an operator's network.

This document is the collection point for all information that effects the functionality or technical requirements for the ESP. As the ESP evolves over time, all modifications to the functionality and design of any ESP in the operator's network should be incorporated into the operator's specific development plans.

Enhanced Services Platform Overview

The Enhanced Services Platform (ESP) will be the point of entry for all incoming calls to the Traditional Telecommunication company. It allows wireless operators to offer their subscribers significant features in addition to voice mail.

The initial requirement for the platform will be to support call management features, as well; it will be the foundation upon which a company offers Telecommunications plans to deploy future services for its subscribers.

The ESP is the solid foundation upon which to build customer applications; hence it requires industrial grade computers with a UNIX based operating system. In addition it offers a range of Voice Response Units (VRUs) and appropriate core software.

In today's PCS environment, the platform needs to support not only voice mail but also voice recognition with a hit rate of better than 70% accuracy.

The author believes that there are four major benefits of the Enhanced Services Platform, which are described as follows:

Ubiquitous Service

The operator's subscribers can have consistent access to services and features from any originating access point (wire or wireless). The subscribers will experience a common "look and feel" when using a wide variety of services.

Rapid Service Development and Deployment

The author believes that with the Computer Telephony Integration application being developed rapidly, companies will be able to differentiate its service offering from its competitors.

Vendor Independence

With the open nature of the platforms and applications which build the foundations of the Enhance Services Platform, operators will be able to introduce new hardware and software elements without relying on a any one vendor.

Service Customization

The Enhanced Services Platform will allow an operator to provide new services to subscribers on a market trial basis. From the trials and through research the service offerings can be enhanced to meet subscriber requirements quickly and effectively.

The ESP will be interfaced to the operator's PCS network, with a direct interface to a switching platform, as well as to various intelligent peripheral, such as voice mail with voice recognition.

ESP Architecture

A typical ESP configuration will consist of the following components which comprise the core;

- Matrix Switch
- Application Processor (AP)
- Voice Response Units (VRU)
- Voicemail Server (VS)

The architecture of the ESP is designed in such a manner as to provide as efficient performance as possible based on the restrictions of the switching supplier infrastructure. Figure 5 shows a typical graphical representation of the ESP architecture.

The architecture can also take advantage of advanced signaling protocols residing in the switch.

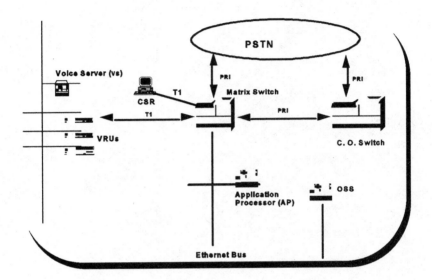

Figure 5: Enhanced Services Platform Architecture

All communications between the matrix switch, Applications Processor (AP), and Voice Response Units (VRU) can be via an Ethernet ThinNet bus.

The VRUs can use an independent Ethernet bus for storing and retrieving voice messages and prompts from the Voice Server. Based on the traffic requirements for the operator's subscribers, the voice server configuration over a bus configuration will allow the best performance for voice retrieval.

5

Introduction to Operational Support Systems (OSS)

The Operations System Support (OSS) Team is normally responsible for delivering solutions that provide a link between Network Elements and Billing Systems (otherwise known as Business Systems). These solutions are classified as Operations (or Operational) Support Systems and specifically address Service Fulfillment and Message Processing business needs.

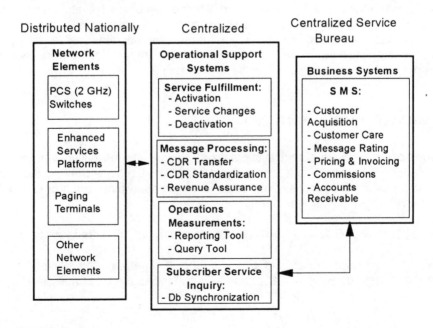

Figure 6: OSS Message Processing

Operations System Support (OSS) provides a flexible link between the Billing Systems and the Network Elements. The OSS isolates the Billing and customer care Systems from the Network Elements. The two main functions performed by OSS are:

Service Fulfillment: Receiving customer and service information from the Business System, adding network programming information and passing the information to the Network Elements for service activation, deactivation or changes.

Message Processing: Extracting call detail records (CDR) from the Network Elements, performing matching of related CDRs, standardizing the CDRs and sending them to the Billing System for pricing and invoicing.

Traditionally, OSS has also included other support systems such as repair management systems, workforce management systems, etc.

The operator's key business objectives supported by the OSS include:

- Be a low cost and quick provider of new product and services
- Accommodate network changes effectively and efficiently

OSS will enable the operator to meet these objectives by minimizing major modifications to the customer acquisition and billing system as new products and services are introduced. As well, in the future, if the operator decides to replace the billing system, there would be no major impact to Network systems supporting provisioning and message processing.

Service Fulfillment

An operator has to select a specialized supplier as the billing vendor. The supplier's Subscriber Management System (SMS) will provide the operators with a computerized based service order entry screens that supports Customer Acquisition and Customer Care.

The purpose of OSS is to provide operators with an automated facility to:

- Provision subscribers' phone on the PCS network immediately.
- Upgrade subscribers' phone with enhanced services immediately.

Business Requirements

This section typically describes the operator's provisioning business requirements for both the Subscriber Management System (SMS) and the Operations Support System (OSS).

Alternatives

Eight (8) provisioning alternatives are normally identified for launch date. The alternatives to capturing provisioning information include:

- OSS user interfaces.
- OSS screens are used to capture provisioning information.
- SMS scaled down order entry screens.
- SMS screens are used to capture provisioning information. Only limited contract information is captured during customer contact
- All SMS order entry screens.
- SMS screens are used to capture provisioning information. All customer information is entered during customer contact.
- SMS/OSS order entry screen combination.
- A combination of SMS order entry screens and OSS windows are used to capture provisioning information.

All alternatives are driven by the inventory of leased phones and will require the following:

- Set up all mobile phones in the SMS under an operator account (the agent). Activate at least one (1) Mobile phone with the appropriate interface to the Inventory system.

- System user moves a set of mobile phones from the operator's account to the agent's account. The Subscriber Management System (SMS) will produce a report on the phones that are turned over to agent's phones together with a demo phone attached to the appropriate price plan.

Operators normally prefer the provisioning alternative that requires no data entry duplication and accommodates credit check prior to activating the Mobile handset and Enhanced Services.

Operators normally also prefer that one set of homogeneous user interfaces are provided to CSRs (Customer Service Reps) and as much as possible the CSR does not have to physically toggle between SMS and OSS.

The following demarcation should exist between SMS and OSS:

- SMS to activate customer account, keep track of the inventory, and maintain customer acquisition information such as credit, price plans, products/services, bill cycles, etc.
- OSS to activate services on ESP and PCS. OSS should not duplicate the information residing in the ESP, PCS or SMS repositories.

Message Processing

This section describes the requirements for the Call Detail Record (CDR) Transfer component of the Message Processing system. The CDR Transfer component will retrieve CDRs from the Enhanced Services Platforms (ESPs) and Personal Communications Systems Switches (PCS Switches) in regional offices and deliver them to the billing system. The CDRs will be reformatted from their proprietary formats to a standard format understood by the billing system.

The term "CDR" will be used to define the records for all billable services, such as paging services, not just for incoming and outgoing "calls" as the name implies.

The main objectives of Requirements Analysis are to:

- Ensure the completeness and feasibility of the business requirements.
- Ensure user ownership of the requirements specification.
- Formally document the business requirements to obtain user review and sign-off.
- Develop requirements for the system that can be translated into detailed technical designs.

In this section the business requirements will be broken down into two components. An event model and a process model.

An event model is a description of the application according to external events it must process and respond to. The billing system will process CDRs generated by subscriber's using the operator's telecommunications service platform, including ESPs and PCS Switches.

Both the PCS Switches and the ESP create several different types of CDRs; each of which can represent a different billable call scenario. The event model created for this report will attempt to describe the CDRs created by the PCS Switches and the ESP and the relevant details that will differentiate call scenarios.

A process or functional model describes all the processes necessary for the system to meet the business requirements. The process model for this component of the Message Processing system will describe all the steps necessary to transfer CDRs from the network elements to the OSS Host, reformat and filter CDRs, and transfer the standard CDRs on to the Billing system.

ESP CDRs

The ESP CDRs describe network events that do not necessarily correspond to billable CDRs. Each ESP service that will be billed is made up of one or more network events. Network events describe things like: incoming call, incoming call hang up, or call forwarded to a VRU.

Each outgoing or incoming call processed by the ESP will produce at least two CDRs, one for call initiation and the other for call termination. If the call is transferred to a VRU or other device, the billable CDR could be made up of three or more ESP events.

There are several events that the ESP keeps track of. Typically, the following eleven events (associated numbers in parenthesis) are logged as CDRs on the ESP:

1. **Incoming call:** Calls that connect to the ESP by a subscriber dialing their voice mail directly or a PCS handled call which is transferred to the ESP because the phone is busy, not answered, or not found by the PCS Network.

2. **Incoming call hang-up:** The event that occurs when the caller/subscriber hangs up from an ESP session. This includes the time when a caller calls a mobile phone, it's busy, it rolls over to the subscriber's voice mail, and the caller hangs up before leaving a message.

3. **Callback start:** The event that occurs when a subscriber begins a callback when in their voicemail session.

4. **Callback result:** This logs whether the callback was successfully connected with the called party or not.

5. **Callback end:** The event that occurs when a subscriber ends a callback when in their voicemail session.

6.   **Call forwarded to switch:** All incoming mobile calls are routed through the ESP and forwarded to the switch. If a caller dials a mobile subscriber, the ESP will forward the call to the switch. If the call rolls over to voicemail, it will be transferred to the ESP. In terms of ESP CDRs, the only call event that will not trigger this CDR to be created is if the ESP call centre number is called directly, and thus the switch is not used.

7.   **Call forwarded to mbox**: The event that occurs when a call comes into the ESP and is connected with the subscriber's mailbox.

8.   **Page sent:** This event occurs when a direct page or paging notification takes place. The second data field in this event will determine if the page was generated by the paging notification or not. The first data field after the event number always has the pager number that was used for the page. The second data field will always be the call center number if the page was sent via paging notification. If the page was a direct page, this field will hold the data entered by the caller (i.e., phone number or message).

9.   **Call forwarded to customer service:** This event occurs when a subscriber in a voicemail administration session hits the correct number to connect them to the operator's customer service center. The voicemail session will automatically end after the call to customer service is over.

10.   **Caller logs into mailbox:** This event occurs when a subscriber calls their own mobile number or the call centre number to log into their own mailbox.

11.   **Caller left message:** This event occurs when a caller leaves a message in a subscriber's voice mailbox.

Other information that the ESP logs for CDRs that is important to determine billable CDR information includes:

■   **GMT time** indicates the time of the event in UNIX time. This is the number of seconds since January 1, 1970 GMT. To determine duration, this field will have to be compared against the start and stop time of the event (e.g., callbacks).

■   **Call_tid** indicates that the event was part of a particular call or voicemail session. All events that occur in the same call or session will have the same call_tid.

■   **Dialed digits** indicates the dialed digits for all calls, pages, and callbacks.

■ **PID** indicates the subscriber that is registered on the ESP. This information must be present in order to identify the subscriber that is responsible to pay for the variable usage of the ESP platform and its corresponding services. In all but one scenario, the PID will be present in the group of CDRs that belong to the same call or session (i.e., call_tid).

When a call is made to a handset which connects (i.e., does not roll over to voicemail) and subsequently ends, the PID is not logged by the ESP. This is not important as this scenario represents duplicate information (CDRs) that the PCS Network Elements will keep track of. For all other ESP scenarios, the PID will be logged in the second data field of either or both of the "call forwarded to mbox" or "caller logs into mailbox" events.

Statistical Processing and Reporting

Several departments within an operator organization, including Engineering Planning and Marketing, normally request detailed reports on calling patterns and network usage in order to help them complete their jobs more effectively and efficiently. These statistics can be captured from CDRs, and Operational Measurements (OMs).

Engineering Planning must design the network to provide sufficient coverage for the operator subscribers while keeping capital investment at a minimum.

It is crucial that this group get accurate and timely information on how the network is being used by the operator's customers. If reports on subscriber calling patterns and OMs are being prepared manually, then this is time consuming, inefficient, and expensive.

One of Marketing's main roles is to understand how the subscriber base is using each service in order to target and price the operator's offering effectively.

This group must understand statistics such as busy hours, average call duration, calls transferred to voicemail, and number/duration of callbacks. These statistics can be gathered from the CDRs that are transferred from the Network Elements.

After the CDRs are converted into a standard CDR, statistics will be captured and stored in a database on the OSS Host Computer. In the same processing stream, the standard CDRs will be transferred to the Billing system. In a separate processing stream OMs will be transferred from the switches to the OSS Host computer.

Statistics important to Engineering Planning and Design could then be captured and stored in the same database as the CDR statistics. As these hourly statistics are being stored in the OSS Host Computer, users in various organizations within the company could perform adhoc queries or use "canned" reports to get the information they need.

The following processes will need to be designed and programmed in order fulfill the basic requirements of the Statistics Processing and Reporting component of the Message Processing System:

- Gather and store statistics on standard CDRs.
- Transfer Operational Measurements from the Network Elements to the OSS Host Computer.
- Gather and store statistics on OMs.
- Design and build "canned" reports on network usage and calling patterns.
- Design and build the interface between user "client" computers and the OSS Host Computer in order to allow adhoc queries to the statistics database.

This chapter describes high level requirements for processing Operational and call statistics from the operator's current network. Statistical processing could be included as part of a Message Processing System.

The analysis presented in this document is preliminary; further analysis and interviews with the appropriate user groups is needed.

Data Sources

There two major data sources currently available to collect statistics on the operator's network:

- Switch and ESP Call Detail Records (CDRs).
- Switch Operational Measurements (OMs).

The switch will normally create files each hour for both OMs and CDRs. These hourly files may be transferred using the switch's proprietary protocol or a simple FTP.

Normally, Operational FTPs transfer all CDRs from the switch to the OSS Host, and simply transfers them to the Billing system. No automated process exists today to retrieve OMs. The ESP should be creating hourly CDR files or at best in real time. A simple RCP utility could be used to transfer ESP CDRs to the OSS Host for message processing purposes.

Requirements Analysis

CDR Statistics

Both Marketing and Engineering normally request summary reports on call data from the OSS team. There are two major requirements:

- Analysis of Call Patterns: Both Marketing and Engineering would like to understand what type of calls are popular at what time during the day. They would like to analyze busy hours and call patterns to learn more about how their customers are using the operator's services.

- Analysis of Call Routing/Destinations: In order for Engineering to understand how to optimally design the network, they need to analyze how the subscriber's are using the operator's physical network. They would like to analyze what parts of the network are being used most frequently by the operator's subscribers.

The following list shows the specific data they have requested:

1.   Number of calls by type: SWITCH CDR types include Incoming calls, Outgoing calls, Voicemail transfers, OTAR calls, Service Inquiries, Emergency calls. ESP CDR types include Voicemail Administration, Deposits, Callbacks, Transfers to Customer Service, Direct Pages, or Pages by Notification. Some of these service types will be more important than others, incoming and outgoing calls for example.

2.   Average duration of calls: SWITCH and ESP CDRs either provide duration or give enough information to calculate it.

3.   Number of calls by Destination: ESP and SWITCH CDRs show the dialed digits for each outgoing call. The NPA/NXX could be parsed out the dialed digits field and mapped to a table that had Local Calling Area, or city for each NPA/NXX.

4.   Number of calls by Route: SWITCH CDR shows DN2, or the number of the communication lines for the MSC used to deliver the call. This is the closest thing possible to "route". In a Cellular network, apparently more information is given on the CDR for a route.

5.   Average interval between calls: This requirement may be difficult to produce depending on what Marketing is precisely looking for.

6.   <u>Data by Hour, Day, Week</u> - The above data should be shown in different time increments to view statistical patterns over time.

There are also requirements to see combinations of the above information, such as number of calls per route and average call duration per route.
To cover much of the call pattern analysis, a report (see below) could be put together each day:

97/01/01 Hour	Inc. Calls	Avrg. Dur.	Out Calls	Avrg. Dur.	Total Calls	Avrg. time
00:00	100	2:00	200	2:30	2000	2:10
01:00	110	2:30	300	2:40	2500	2:30
....						
23:00	120	2:20	400	3:10	3500	2:10
Totals	3000	2:25	4000	2:45	40000	2:05

Other services such as Emergency calls, Voicemail administration, callbacks, and pages could be provided in this table.

A report such as the one above would allow Marketing and Engineering to analyze call patterns and busy hours. An aggregate of these reports could be put together for a week or month to give Marketing and Engineering a higher level understanding of the call patterns.

The challenge to the OSS teams to fulfill these call statistics requirements is to collect enough data in an efficient manner. As the list of requirements is reviewed above, it can be seen that a large amount of data may need to be collected and stored in order to create these reports. An efficient data structure will be required in order for the Engineers and Marketers to create adhoc reports easily.

OM Statistics

The operator's current mobile network provides Operational Measurements (OMs) in an hourly file, such as the CDR files. The requirements for detailed network statistics will be driven by Network Operations and Engineering groups. The following list shows the main OM groups:

- **Account Management:** This holds information on CDRs statistics, data packet information, and file management alarms.

- **Authentication:** This holds information on the challenge/response pairs that are generated by the system when a subscriber is attempting to verify that their portable is authorized to use the service.

- **Call Processing:** This holds information on how calls terminate, how calls are blocked, X.25 packet communication, and other statistics on how calls are treated.

- **Home Location Register:** This holds information on how HLR and Visitor Location Record (VLR) data is used and transferred throughout the network.

- **Mobility Link:** This hold statistics on communication between the SWITCH and PSTN.

- **OTAR Management:** This holds information on the OTAR packet communication when subscriber's phones are being authenticated for each call.

- **Zone Processing:** This a large OM group which hold information on Radio call processing, zone account management, zone call processing, zone fault management, zone mobility link processing, zone subscriber management, and zone time of day management.

One of the main problems with the OMs that are normally available with the mobile network is that the documentation provided with Operational Measurements is not detailed enough. In many instances, it is difficult to understand how these statistics are generated or "pegged" in the network. It is crucial in making network design decisions that these OMs are understood in detail.

The main OM groups that Engineering are interested in are the Call and Zone Processing groups.

Regardless of the PCS or Cellular Technology that the operator has, it is very important that Operational Measurements are transferred and reported on as part of the OSS Message Processing System. Engineering and Operations will rely on analyzing these statistics in order to optimally design the network.

6

Introduction to Network Management Systems

Overview

Network Management has traditionally been the last item to be planned when designing networks. A system that can provide data and voice interconnectivity may appear to meet all of its objectives, but if it cannot be managed, it soon becomes worthless.

Companies require uninterrupted flow of business applications and information across their networks and to ensure this, network management systems have become integral parts of any computer environment.

The main function of any network is to consistently satisfy business requirements and only through network management can this aim be met. The function of a network manager is to ensure the goals of an organization are met.

Networks can be privately owned, leased from a public operator, or fully private. The transmission media can be copper, optical or radio based. The network can be analogue or digital and can carry a mix of services.

A typical heterogeneous environment consists of a wide variety of network combinations which the management system has to operate.

In addition, within the above types of networks, there exists an equally wide spread of equipment needing management.

There will be a mix of interfaces, some standard and some non-standard Modern devices have a certain amount of intelligence to allow for more sophisticated management functions while older equipment have primitive management capabilities, and there is a mix of vendor equipment. All of these need to be managed as one unit.

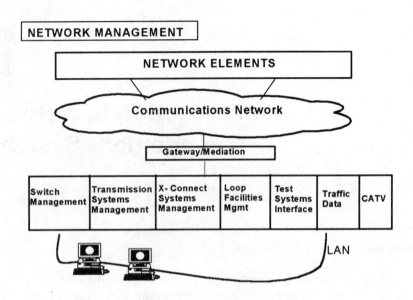

Figure 7: Network Management Elements

Because there are so many different elements to manage, network management is slowly moving from function oriented solutions toward process oriented solutions.

Focus is shifting to managing the entire enterprise which requires a much more intelligent network able to determine potential faults in the computing enterprise and be able to take autonomous action to prevent them from impacting the user.

The platform characteristics of a comprehensive open systems solution should include:

- Multi-vendor/Multi-technology support.
- Multi-protocol/Multi-message format support.
- Open Client/Server architecture.
- Separation of functionality according to ITU-TS TMN layers.
- Significant use of network intelligence.
- Based on Object Orient Technology.
- Scalability easy addition of computing resources.
- High Reliability.
- High Performance.
- Expandable for future services and network technologies.

The International Standards Organization (ISO) has classified network management functions into 5 groups: fault management, configuration management, performance management, security management and accounting management.   Functions, such as alarm detection, capacity management, network access control, etc., are categorized into their appropriate process group.   These function groups will be discussed in more detail in the section Network Infrastructure.

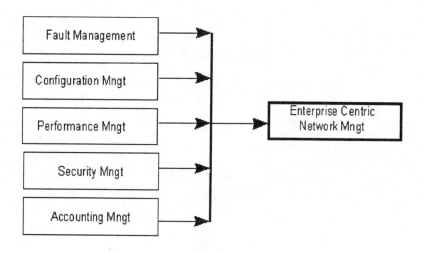

Figure 8: Network Management Functions

The operator may be building a heterogeneous network using a wide variety of equipment, protocols, applications, interfaces, transmission methods, and standards.   Every element in the network needs to be managed, and what makes the task even more difficult is the fact that the operator's network may be nationwide.

The design of the operator's network management structure is key to how efficiently it manages all the different and wide spread components.   Bandwidth is expensive and it may not be in the operator's best interest to backhaul all management information to one site.   A centrally owned distributed management structure is usually recommended for Wide Area Networks.

What an operator does not want is to implement a management station for every vendor whose equipment is installed in the computing environment.   Ideally, a management system able to communicate with all network elements and present management information in a uniform manner using a graphical user interface (GUI) is preferred.

Traditionally, equipment manufacturers have been following a "box-centric" approach where as a network management station is allocated for each hardware unit rather than an "enterprise-centric" approach where a single station controls the complete network including all aspects of hardware, software, monitoring, maintenance and statistical reporting.

The operator's Network Management System (NMS) needs to interface directly with the following elements:

- SS7 Management System.
- RF Management System.
- Base Station Controllers, Base Station Subsystem Management System.
- HLR/VLR/AUC Management Systems.
- Channel Bank and Multiplexer Management Systems (such as the Newbridge 4602).
- Microwave Management System.
- OSS Management System.
- ESP Management System.
- MSC Managing System (Switch).
- Alarm and Surveillance Management System.

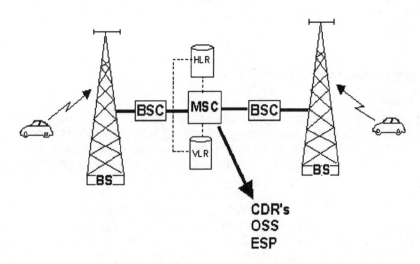

Figure 9: Component Management

Network Management strategies, trends, standards, and architectures will be discussed in more detail in the following sections.

Design of Network Management System

Network Management Structure

Network Management hierarchy is usually based on geographical location and span of control. Management distribution is thought of as local, regional, national and international. Once distance becomes a factor, management becomes crucial. The greater the distance, more and varied equipment (i.e., circuits, switches, services. modems) need to be monitored and controlled to provide uninterrupted information flow.

The following diagram depicts the two strategies that an operator may be considering for distributing network management:

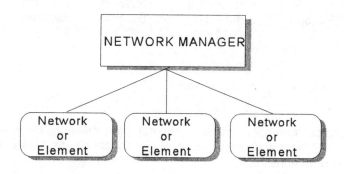

Figure 10: Centralized Network Management

In centralized management all management functions are carried out at one location usually by a powerful server. This will serve a small network but will become more difficult with larger networks due to the distances involved.

All managed objects are carried over the same links that data travels over and if a problem arises, bandwidth can quickly become congested. Wide area bandwidth is expensive.

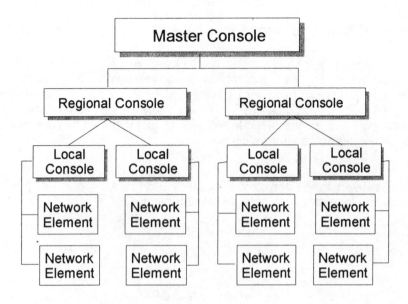

Figure 11: Hierarchical Network Management

With hierarchical management the local manager monitors the immediate alarms and problems and sends only major or critical alarms back to either a regional or central console.

This cuts down on management messages having to travel any distances and also allows for faster response time for the user or resource experiencing the problem. This structure avoids the issue of bringing down the whole management system since it is distributed. There is no "single point of failure".

Network Management Functions

It was established earlier that a network management system's function is to ensure the efficient and reliable delivery of an organization's network services. In order to manage this, there must be something in place to measure the performance of the network against, a sort of "benchmark". This is not easy to define.

Some indicators of a well designed network are:

1.   High level of service/availability: This is two-fold in that network availability can be measured against down-time/month while level of service is user subjective.

2.   Efficient network utilization: Bandwidth can be under utilized in which case there is waste or bandwidth can be over utilized which means that the network is suffering from congestion and delays.

3.   Uninterrupted information (data or voice) flow: This is easy to measure but the challenge is to avoid failed communications, errors, and to deliver the information on a timely basis (i.e., user acceptable response time).

Fault management involves the detection, diagnosis, and correction of network faults. The management system should be able to pin-point the exact location of the fault within the network and zoom in to any level required (i.e., circuit on a card).

Diagnostics of this type is also required for remote sites, especially if a technician needs to be dispatched. This way, the technician is able to come prepared with the right equipment.

Fault management must also provide the opportunity to react proactively to network problems and alert users to potential delays or degradation in service before it actually occurs.

Elements managed include:

■   Automatic alarm detection and corrective action.
■   Complete alarming capabilities for various set-points, thresholds and configuration discrepancies.
■   Trouble ticketing.

All the above elements monitor a defined set of management variables.

Configuration management provides a mechanism for managing network nodes or "objects" which are under the control of the management system. Configuration management includes starting managed objects, shutting down managed objects, collecting state information, and controlling services depending on user/application demand.

Configuration management allows the management system to dynamically change an object's parameters or set up an alternative route through the network. The management principle also manages and changes to any network configuration be it system or element level. It also includes electronic software distribution or the ability to download information through the network.

Managed network components:

1.   Define multi-level view of the network.
2.   Maintain a complete inventory of all wide area network components that comprise the network.
3.   Manage and coordinate network moves, additions, changes, and upgrades.
4.   Provide documentation updates.

Performance management involves monitoring the performance of systems throughout the network enterprise.

This includes gathering statistical information about managed objects in order to analyze and predict trends in the network. Statistical analysis will assist in re-designing the network to reflect the established trends. There must also be a method of filtering all the statistical information gathered, otherwise the management system will be swamped with data.

Performance tasks include:

- Real-time monitoring and historical trending.
- Capacity management.
- Annual network audit: an objective assessment of the network in terms of technology installed, network utilization, network performance and network efficiency.

Security management includes the authentication and authorization of users on the network. Security involves determining who can do what and to what extent. It is described in levels or layers.

Some security functions are:

1.   Implement and manage filter tables for device connectivity to the network.
2.   Implement and control access and privileges to the network components.

Accounting management includes the set of facilities which enables charges to be determined for the use of network resources and the costs allocated to each resource. Accounting management may also include asset and inventory management. This involves keeping track of all network resources, configurations, asset value and ownership.

It could also include:

- Report generation of configuration and performance management deliverables.
- Maintain network availability, mean-time-to-response, and traffic measurements.

Network Management Strategy

Network management needs to change from proprietary based management to standards based management. Today, two different networks from two different vendors are managed by proprietary applications. The two systems cannot communicate and the closest integration of the two is to run them on the same workstation under two separate windows. This still requires human intervention to initiate the applications and to pass any information between them.

The evolution from proprietary to standard interface management would look like the following:

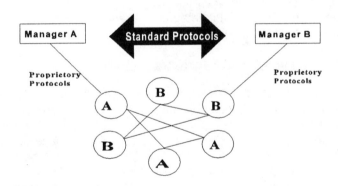

Figure 12: Network Interaction

Network management systems which are geared toward "mono-services" (i.e., telephone network, IP network, SNA network, packet switch network, etc.) need to integrate with each other to satisfy the trend of heterogeneous networks using multi-services.

The management of a network is treated as separate from the management of services carried on the network. These need to be treated as one entity.

Network Management Standards

In the area of network management, the standards committee is based upon the Open System Interconnect Model referred to as the OSI model. Its aim is to allow computers from different manufacturers to talk to each other. Base OSI standards provide standards that can be applied to many different applications

Common Management Information Protocol (CMIP)

Manager and agent applications exchange information using the Common Management Information Protocol (CMIP). It is an object-oriented protocol which means it sends messages about objects. An object is a collection of information which represents a resource or function in the system being managed. Managed objects include "transceivers" or "handover algorithms". Typical messages using CMIP might be "request transceiver A to perform a diagnostic test B".

Management Information Base (MIB)

The set of objects the agent manages is called the Management Information Base (MIB). The MIB contains a virtual image of how the network is working at any time, and by manipulating the image, the management system can access the real database within the node.

Telecommunications Management Network (TMN)

The basic concept behind the TMN is to provide an organized network structure in order to allow interconnection between various types of Operating Systems (OS) and telecommunications equipment using standardized interfaces. This should be applicable to all PCS technologies. This is necessary because currently there is no decision on what technology will form the basis of PCS.

A PCS network environment is unique in that it deploys a large number of transceivers over a widespread area which have to be managed with minimal manual intervention.

The mobility aspect complicates the management of subscriber profiles and the processing of accounting data.

The three main categories in PCS management are:

- Management of Radio Resources.
- Management of Terminal Mobility.
- Management of Personal Mobility.

Data Message Handler (DMH)

This standard is not part of the TMN standard. It provides a way of exchanging usage and rating data across jurisdictions (billing). It was built for exchanging data between cellular network and it is not clear how extensible it is to PCS networks.

Simple Network Management Protocol (SNMP)

Simple Network Management Protocol is used to manage networks which use Transmission Control Protocol and Internet Protocol (TCP/IP) as the transport mechanism. SNMP uses a polling access process and no sessions are maintained between the manager and its managed objects. The rate of polling can be varied to save on bandwidth and response time.

SNMP was designed to be an interim standard until the OSI based network management standards (CMIP) were established and available. SNMP has become popular among several hundred vendors and will probably be around in networks for quite a while.

SNMP is divided into 5 basic message types:

- **GET-REQUEST** is used by the manager to ask for one or more network management variables from an agent MIB.

- **GET-NEXT-REQUEST** has similar functions to GET-REQUEST, but it enables portions of the MIB to be stepped through, and the next variable to be asked for.

- **GET-RESPONSE** is used by the agent to provide the information requested by the manager.

- **SET-REQUEST** is used by the manager to change the value of a MIB object or variable, including booting and re-booting devices.

- **TRAP** is slightly different from the above, since it originates from the managed element and allows them to send events to the manager. It is an unsolicited, asynchronous message sent from the managed agent to the manager, usually about a threshold that has been exceeded. Vendors can add proprietary traps for indicating alarms raised by their equipment.

SNMP and CMIP

The gap between SNMP and CMIP is being bridged by the group called OSI Internet Management (OIM). They are working on developing a protocol for the transition from SNMP to OSI; the transport of CMIP over TCP/IP. This protocol is called CMOT. It is not being implemented by very many and is a fairly unpopular protocol.

<u>Managers and Agents</u>

A management system cannot effectively control a large number of network resources directly, so it employs management agents that run on the nodes to control certain subsets.

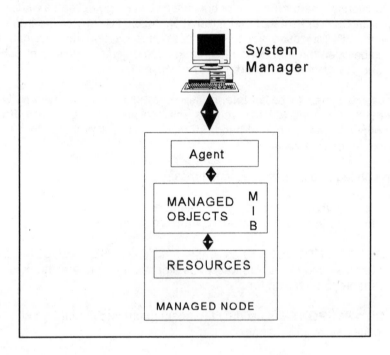

Figure 13: Managed Node

Network Management Systems

Summary

Resources required to maintain the equipment, hardware and software of the management system.   Key elements of support provided for the key infrastructure elements, providing task requirements, and timing: Personnel numbers, skill requirements and training plans.

ARCHITECTURE

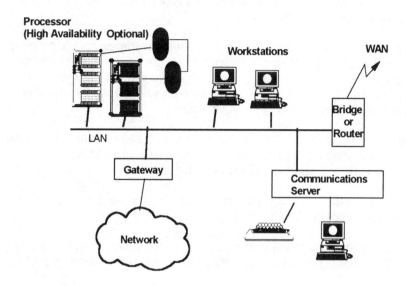

Figure 14: Architecture

Important Issues

Without a decision on management system strategy it is difficult to determine resource requirements. It is assumed the management structure will be a centralized control of the entire network enterprise with limited control given to regions. Local support is also necessary as the business will demand this. Customers will expect immediate resolution to any network problems and failure to do so would be detrimental to the organization.

Skill requirements will depend on the technology implemented.   Most management platforms are UNIX based, so a knowledge of UNIX is required. To lessen the training requirements of 1st level support, the management system will be implemented with a user friendly interface to all management functions and processes.

The GUI must also present all vendor specific management applications in a uniform manner to the operator. The management system needs to interface with various types of equipment and present the collected information in a uniform manner so that the operator is unaware that they are talking to unique network nodes.

The interfaces, signaling protocols, operating systems, and programming languages have to follow established standards. The level of operator skills in the region need to be determined as it will depend on the level of control the regions are given.

Because the 2 GHz network is complex and encompasses a large geographic area, the applied management strategy should be decentralized with centralized control over certain components and configurations of the network. The number of sites and locations of the sites will directly affect the number of tiers implemented in the management structure.

There can be up to 4: Central, Region, Local, and Element. Customers will expect an immediate response to any problem they may be experiencing which requires a local support presence at major sites.

Local management usually includes day-to-day maintenance on network nodes or element level troubleshooting.

Regional management will incorporate local management and filter any alarms or network faults that do not directly concern the overall network performance.

Central management controls the overall network performance. It is interested in all critical or severe alarms/faults that occur in the regions and it will dictate the network configuration and manage all changes to configurations. Network Design & Planning usually resides with central management. Central management is also the off-hours control center

It is the intention of the management system to automate as many tasks as possible and minimize operator intervention with management functions.

Introduction to Billing Systems

Summary

PCS will put new demands on business systems for flexibility, new capabilities and complex interfaces. To meet these demands, the industry will need state-of-the-art systems and supporting architectures. Business systems for PCS will have to be able to support a wide range of new enhanced services, follow-me services and alternate routing capabilities.

The need for customers to add and change services and capabilities "on the fly" will necessitate customer direct access into provisioning and service management systems. New services are likely to require real-time and near real-time processing to a greater extent than ever before.

The focus on security, fraud prevention and the use encryption to stem revenue loss will require business and OSS systems that can perform encryption translation routines and support over the air registration.

Provisioning information, which once moved from the subscriber management system to the network, will now take a reverse path as handsets will automatically be activated at the time of the purchase or first use. New customer information systems must be able to recognize and accommodate this new path.

In addition, the demands for PCS are likely to include multiple new interconnection and roaming arrangements.

This will have significant impact on the ability of the business systems to split revenues on a prorata basis, bill other carriers and reconcile charges from other carriers.

Typically an operator's long-term goal is to bring the billing/customer information system in-house onto a more advanced architecture platform.

However, until revenues and higher customer volumes justify the required expenditure, an operator can support the initiation of PCS service with a Subscriber Management System (SMS), and its existing billing system (running in a service bureau environment).

With some modifications, SMS should be able to manage the services and volumes of the operator's first few years of PCS service. As the changing business needs demand more sophisticated functions, the operator will move toward the capabilities outlined here.

Sales Support/Customer Activation

Systems will allow for real-time activation with the capability for either the salesperson to activate on site or with service information to be the pre-loaded so that customers can activate the handset to be at the time and location of purchase.

Customer activation systems must be supported on point-of-sale terminals for retail sales while a direct field sales force will access a customer activation system through a laptop or hand-held terminal using wireless data communications.

Because service activation may include a large number of customer options and conditions, the Customer Activation System must be designed so that screen navigation is intuitive to a sales representative or CSR and with adequate edits that prevent mistakes.

Customer Care/Customer Information

Customer Information must be maintained in shared or linked databases so that redundancy and synchronization problems do not exist. Likewise, systems should be designed so that data is keyed only once. Where multiple applications use the same data, systems will include electronic interfaces to provide for the download and exchange of information from system to system.

Customer Care Systems will move toward employing graphical user interfaces that allow customer service personnel to access different application environments and different systems with ease and speed.

In addition, when more than one service representative must view the same customer information for a hand-off or trouble-shooting, the Customer Care System will be integrated with the ACD and a local area or wide area network to allow the transfer of a customer record or viewing of a customer record across multiple locations and multiple users. At some future point in time, this may support a "virtual" customer service office.

Given the complex requirements for customizing advanced services, greater control must be placed in the hands of the subscriber for personalizing and maintaining their own services.

Otherwise, the cost of subscriber maintenance will become prohibitive. This will create the need for increasing security around customer and service data with well designed service management systems.

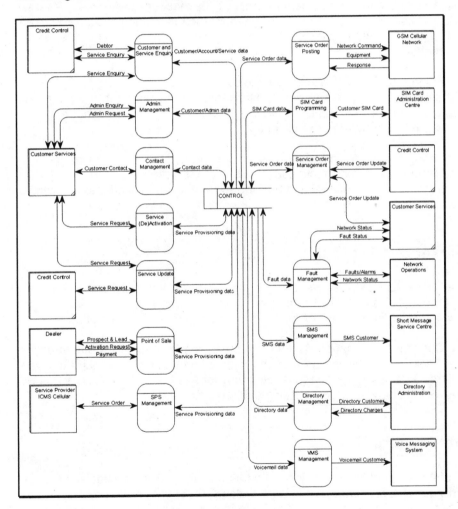

Figure 15: GSM Customer Management Example

With the increased need to manage costs and increase employee productivity, customers will also be given access to balance and payment information either through IVRUs (Interactive Voice Response Units) or through a terminal.

A customer's specific billed and pre-billed information will be downloaded to an operator supplied application residing on the customer's terminal or PC which will give the customer the capability to sort, format and print information according to his or her own specific needs.

The method of batch processing usage information created at the switch site will no longer suffice for the new services that will be introduced with PCS. Roamer calls, per use charges, products designed for the rental and hospitality markets and prepaid services require real-time processing and rating of subscriber usage information.

The billing system must no longer be the bottleneck for introducing new products and services. Product and pricing plans must be supported in flexible billing systems that do not constantly require the intervention of a programmer to create a new product structure or pricing plan.

The billing system must be designed to support rapid response to competition and first-to-market product introduction with a user-interface that allows a product manager to define variables and perform "what-if" scenarios prior to finalizing a product plan.

Market and Profitability Analysis

The increased competitiveness of the North American market, and the accompanying probability of narrower profit margins, means the carriers must stay on top of the success or failure of products, promotions and programs.

The Customer Information System and the Billing System linked with effective cost tracking capabilities provide the core for an efficient marketing analysis system. Again, information must be timely for it to be useful. This means we must rethink how we process billing and customer account information.

Architecture

All of these capabilities will depend on an architecture that recognizes a close working relationship between business systems, OSS and network systems. The barriers between these systems must be torn down so that data flow efficiently between the multiple components.

Conclusion

As a new company, the operator "A" will have significant requirements for new systems and automated support. Given the level of investment that will be needed to support these requirements, the operator "A" will prioritize those business systems projects that enhance revenues or provide substantial efficiencies.

The existing billing/customer information system will support PCS service initiation. Components can be replaced or enhanced as funds become available and service support warrants. An early priority is likely to be replacement of the user interface portions of the system which are unwieldy and not user-friendly.

In addition, some interfaces must be re-designed to be more efficient (e.g., between the Subscriber Management System and OSS Provisioning) and new electronic interfaces must be built to support billing and provisioning, including links between a Site Management System and SMS (Billing) and between SMS and the future financial system.

The existing interface between SMS and OSS will have to be enhanced to accommodate new services and to provide the data required by the HLR, VLR and SCPs.

A wireless operator's approach to business systems development for PCS should remain focused on controlling costs while at the same time recognizing that effective systems and system links contribute to greater productivity and a work force with the information at hand for planning, decision-making and providing better service to customers.

Issues

External Issues

Interoperability. What will be the requirements to activate and validate subscribers from another carrier? What level of subscriber data must be maintained?

Roaming. What are the requirements to send subscriber information to a centralized database? Exchange of CDRs? Will PCS use a clearinghouse or have bi-lateral agreements? At what point will file formats, record layouts and protocols be standardized for exchange of data?

International roaming. Will roaming need to be supported outside of North America? What provisions must be made for transfer of data, both to validate customers and to bill customers?

Interconnection and Settlements. What will the access charge structure be for interconnection to PSTN? What balancing, reconciliation and audit capabilities are needed? Will operator "A" be allowed reciprocal charges to the PSTN for terminating calls on operator's "A" network?

Equal Access. Will operator "A" be required to provide equal ease of access to all interexchange carriers? What will access charge structure be? Will a CABS-type system be required to bill IXCs for EEA?

Fraud liability. Fraud control is the number one issue for providers of both the current cellular products and the growing PCS market. Fraudulent calls currently cost cellular service providers $1 billion per year in North America.

Aside from some very sophisticated computer-based detection systems, there are two main ways to stop the problem -- personal identification numbers and speaker verification. Both require an additional step for the end user. A third solution, utilizing encryption, does exist but requires extensive modification to both the telephones and supporting system(s).

Will fraud liability follow arrangements put in place in the cellular industry with the home carrier assuming the risk? What requirements will be placed on the foreign carrier to minimize exposure?

Partner Issues

Maintenance, support and transfer of billing data for shared accounts. Will customer/subscriber data be maintained individually by each carrier or in a centralized database? Countrywide specific requirements must be taken into account, including taxation, postal codes, bilingual invoices (if applicable) and inserts.

Preferred roaming arrangements and pricing. Do separate pricing structures need to be maintained for partners? Will this be one structure and the same prices for all partners or partner-specific structures? Partner-specific prices? Would they be a clearinghouse for Canadian, U.S. or International PCS, and will data exchange be handled through a clearinghouse or directly?

Shared resources. Can Business Systems resources be shared? To what extent—shared analysis, shared development, shared software and hardware?

Legal constraints. Do any legal or regulatory impediments exist for data exchange or use of US facilities for a Canadian carrier or a European Union with a Non- European Union carrier?

Company Issues

Real-time call data collection and near-real-time rating. How soon will company products and services require real-time processing? What is the best solution for an architecture to support this—through adjunct processors at switch sites or electronic transmission to central location?

Real-time data collection and analysis may be required to monitor for fraud, credit watch or to monitor for thresholds for other reasons but real-time rating may be required for certain services only.

Real-time activations. What will be the capabilities of the new network? Will the company's switch be able to support this with multi-tasking rather than sequential processing? How can the customer activations application be designed to direct provisioning information to multiple network nodes efficiently and in real-time?

Interface to switch (or HLR) for hotlining. What Billing/Customer Information systems support timely analysis and monitoring for transferring intercept messages to the Network? Will the Network be able to support intercept and transfer to IVRU or the Customer Service group?

Fraud management. How will it differ from analogue cellular fraud? What detection/analysis capabilities exist in the market for digital systems? How quickly can information exchange be established with other carriers to minimize exposure to subscription fraud? With call-back/call-through capabilities in enhanced services platforms, will fraud management need to be incorporated to prevent unauthorized "break-ins?"

Enhanced services. How will enhanced services impact processing requirements for activations and call data collection? How will increased volume of data affect performance of business systems? Network capabilities such as SS#7 and IS-41 allow enhanced services to traverse interconnecting networks, but what will be the billing arrangements for enhanced services when an interconnecting carrier is involved?

New billing capabilities. Billing systems will have to support new billing options including calling party pays, pay per use calling features, and advice of charging and bill per event to credit card. What usage parameters will have to be supported in addition to time and distance of traditional Telecom billing systems (e.g., data packets, characters, page equivalents (for fax), messages, database access and/or changes)?

Customer control and access. Given the complexities of enhanced and advanced services supported through the intelligent network, what capabilities exist for allowing customers to control their own activations, changes, routing options, etc.; for protecting the operator's subscriber and billing data; for capturing data required to assist and bill customers related to customer direct access; and for allowing customer service intervention and reset when a customer has become confused or forgotten information.

Automated Alternate Billing

Automated alternate billing is becoming a requirement as the people-in-motion market looks for other ways to bill and track calls. Providers also see it as a way to open new markets. These markets include travelers, transportation vehicles such as rental cars, buses and taxis, and also high credit risk individuals. This is also a way to secure brand loyalty by attaching value or discounts to the billing credit or debit card.

The methods of payment in such a system include debit card or account, smart card, credit card, and telco calling card. These services act like a commercial point-of-sale terminal as well as a telecommunications device.

Most of these functions require a sub-system to perform a check at a database. If the credit account or debit value is acceptable, the call is allowed to complete. This is not functionally different from the speaker verification example. In fact, it could use speaker verification if additional credit or debit value has to be established. The verification record can reside either on the card or in the system. The card or account can also hold preferences such as carrier, frequently called numbers, or billing options.

We may also find wireless telephones in vending machines at airports, other transportation terminals, hotels, stadiums, and other public places. Users would insert cash or a credit/ debitcard into a slot in the vending machine and a predefined limit would be established for that phone. The limit could be raised but the user would need to interact with an IVR application to arrange for more credit or debit value.

To accomplish this, the same architecture as discussed above would be used. If the user's time on the vending machine phone is about to run out she would be notified while connected to the cellular network. When the cellular user connects with the Mobile Transport Switching Office (MTSO), the MTSO would route the call to the Signal Computing System Architecture (SCSA) platform for *verification of the user's time balance.

This verification could be handled by a local database or a remote database. If the user's cellular time had run out or if the time was running low, the SCSA platform would ask the user if they would like to purchase more time. The user's credit card information would be re-validated against a local or remote database and the call would be returned along with the updated time allotment to the Mobile Transport Switching Office (MTSO).

8

Network Infrastructure

Introduction to Switching Infrastructure

Summary

The switching platform (Mobile Switching Centre) manages the connectivity between the PCS base stations and the various network (LEC, IEC, Private, Signaling, Intelligent Networks, etc.) elements. The switching platform will be engineered to support the anticipated traffic loading of various call types including mobile to land, land to mobile, mobile to mobile, data, and others.

- Switching design has evolved over the past 50 years as a result of improvements in technology, the need to minimize costs and to provide increasingly sophisticated services.

- The move to digital technology has resulted in the use of new communications techniques for directing information flow within a network and has resulted in a significant change in the methods of providing service.

When evaluating the switching platform and related switching infrastructure, key areas to research include:

1. Switch Architecture: Evaluation of the overall structure of the switching platform, including investigation into the core and network architectures as well as peripheral equipment and interconnectivity. Special attention should be placed on redundancy schemes, modularity, and evolution paths and plans.

2. Operational Interfaces: The ability to interact with the MSC to perform service and maintenance functions. These typically include the Man Machine Interface (MMI) as well as any and all associated data interfaces.

3.   Software: Evaluation of the software structure to determine short-term and long-term requirements and capabilities for dealing with software maintenance and system upgrades.

4.   Signaling: Evaluation of signaling capabilities and associated architecture required to support current and next generation signaling functionality. Key areas of concentration include common channel signaling (SS7) capability for future Intelligent Network applications as well as general network interconnectivity.

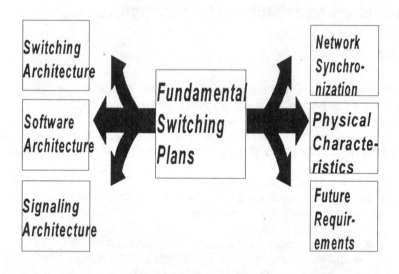

Figure 16: Switching Infrastructure

5.   Network Synchronization: Reviewing the role of the switching platform in providing synchronization to network elements.

6.   Physical Characteristics: Review and evaluation of power and distribution requirements, environmental considerations, hardware considerations, and floor space requirements.

7.   Fundamental Switching Plans: Including routing, numbering, as well as associated traffic engineering concepts.

8.   Future Requirements: Brief evaluation needs to focus on the capability of the switching platform to support future technologies including Asynchronous Transport Mode (ATM) and Advanced Intelligent Network applications.

The switching platform requires extensive study and evaluation as it is typically the backbone of the entire PCS network. Features and functionality provided by the switch will be the basis for the global PCS service offering as provided by the operator's as well as other PCS service providers.

Thorough research needs to be completed not only on the features and functionality of the key MSC vendors platforms (AT&T, NORTEL, Ericsson), but on how the various platforms can be combined and integrated into the operators PCS network (i.e., multi-vendor applications).

Network Element Overview

Summary

The generally accepted network reference model for a cellular telephone network is the TR45 Network Reference Model as shown below in Figure 14.   It represents the theoretical functional entities and their associated interface points that may logically comprise a PCS/cellular network.

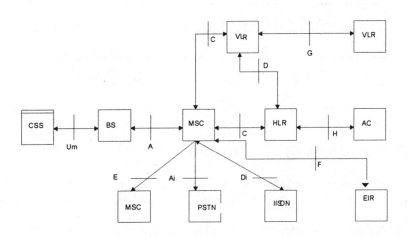

Figure 17: TR45 Network Reference Model

MSC (Mobile Switching Center)

The Mobile Switching Center will typically have the normal capabilities of a telephone exchange (central office) such as call setup, routing selection, switching between incoming and outgoing channels, and control of communications and release of connections. In addition it will handle functions unique to mobile telephone, such as location registration, paging, transfer of encryption data, radio resource management, and call handover between MSCs.

The MSC contains the following interfaces and communicating components:

COMMUNICATING COMPONENTS	INTERFACE NAME
MSC and BSS	A- interface
MSC and PSTN	PSTN interface
MSC and OMC	OMC interface
Network nodes (listed below):	**MAP interface (specific interfaces listed below):**
MSC and VLR	B interface
MSC and HLR	D interface
MSC and DMS-MSC	
MSC and EIR	E interface
HLR and VLR	F interface
VLR and VLR	G interface

Figure 18: Communicating Components and Interfaces

HLR (Home Location Register)

The HLR is responsible for holding the current location and the master parameters of mobile subscribers. The HLR provides the following functionality:

1.   A centralized and master database for all subscriber information
2.   Location services/mobility management
3.   Service initiation/validation.

The HLR can reside as an integrated MSC/HLR component within a small

network environment.   Typically, the HLR will reside as a standalone unit
servicing many hundreds of thousands of subscribers.

VLR (Visitor Location Register)

The visitor location register contains dynamic subscriber information about
activities of a mobile user as they remain within the boundary of the VLR. Its
main function is to facilitate mobility management within a specified boundary
(i.e., within all base stations connected to that MSC).

As a user crosses VLR boundaries, the HLR manages the transition of the data.
The VLR provides the following functionality:

1.   Mobility management
2.   Temporary mobile user data storage and management
3.   Authentication support

The VLR is typically co-located within the MSC platform; however, it can also
be moved to an off board platform to allow for higher performance of the MSC.
Normally, a VLR can hold up to 300,000 subscribers.

AC (Authentication Center)

The AC generates security related parameters used to ensure that only
authorized mobile subscribers have the ability to access the network. Note that
in typical North American cellular applications the AC is not utilized.

EIR (Equipment Identity Register)

The EIR provides configuration, monitoring, and control of the equipment identity
database. This master database is used by the PCS network as part of the
subscriber/terminal authentication process. It allows the PCS operator to reduce
the fraud often associated with wireless networks. Note that in typical North
American cellular applications the EIR is not utilized.

BSS (Base Station Subsystem Overview)

The BSS is typically known as the combination between the BSC (Base Station
Controller and the BTS (Base Transceiver Station).

The BSS may perform some or all of the following tasks using TCE, BCE and
BTS components (see below for descriptions):

1.   Channel configuration
2.   Channel management for traffic and signaling channels
3.   Channel coding and decoding
4.   Transcoding and speed adaptation of data
5.   Handover management for passing on connections in the BSS
6.   Encryption
7.   Frequency hopping management (if applicable)
8.   Antenna diversity
9.   OA&M functions
10.   Signaling functions

The BSS will typically include the following elements:

- BSC
- BTS

BSC (Base Station Controller)

The Base Station Controller manages the cells. In this function, the primary activity is in subscriber mobility management. On information received from the mobile, the BSC makes the decision as to when and to which cell the mobile will hand over. This architecture will typically reduce the load placed upon the MSC.

The BSC typically provides interface to the MSS (Mobile Switching System) and supplies central intelligence of every BSS. It can typically be broken into TCE (Transcoding Equipment) and BCE (BSS Central Equipment).

The TCE has the task of adapting different transmission rates for speech and data. Encoded speech signals in the BSS are compressed for transmission back to the MSC where they will be mixed back to the original channels.

BCE is typically the central intelligence of BSS. It provides switching, operating and maintenance functions for several BTS (Base Transceiver Station).

BTS (Base Transceiver Station)

The BTS is responsible for supplying the individual radio zones with transmission channels; they provide the "Um" interface (also known as the "Air" interface) between the network and the mobile subscriber.

CSS (Cellular Subscriber Station)

The Cellular Subscriber Station is the radio equipment used by the subscriber to access the cellular system.

Physical Overview

The PCS system's large flexibility enables the operator to easily increase the equipment capacity, according to traffic needs. The number of links needed to connect the various system units together is variable, and depends on the amount of traffic that must be handled.

BTS

The BTS includes a base cabinet and one or more extension cabinets except for Micro-BTS. The amount of extension cabinets depends on the number of radio channels to be supported and on the site structure (monocellular or multicellular site). The same flexibility applies to transceiver units inside each cabinet.

There are two types of BTS mostly manufactured by nearly all suppliers:

- The Mini-BTS for outdoor and indoor installations
- The Standard BTS and Micro-BTS for indoor installations

BSC

The BSC normally includes a control cabinet and an equipment cabinet. The amount of constituent modules in each cabinet depends on the number of PCM links to be managed. There are several types of BSC depending on the amount of traffic to be managed.

TCU

A TCU cabinet manufactured for example by NORTEL is normally composed of four shelves. Each shelf manages four PCM links from the MSC and one from the BSC. The number of shelves depends on the number of required PCM links to connect the BSC to the MSC. Other manufacturers may follow different physical designs.

MEU, DLNA

The MEU and DLNA are normally both housed in a unit fixed on a mast, installed close to the antenna, at less than 5 meters (16 feet 5 inches).

Functional Overview

The PCS network is a versatile, open-ended digital radio-telephone system. It has been designed to reduce not only installation costs, but also network operating costs, especially transmission ones.

The mobile radio-telephone system includes the following subsystems, as specified in international technical recommendations:

- The Base Station Subsystem (BSS).
- The Network Subsystem (NSS).
- The Operations and Maintenance Subsystem (OMS), including a radio Operations and Maintenance Center (OMC-R) and a NSS Operations and Maintenance Center (OMC-S).

The PCS/cellular subsystems are described in the following section. Three main laws ruled their design:

- Include all cellular system features leading to an optimal radio engineering.
- Minimize network operating costs, especially the cost of terrestrial links and installation costs provide an efficient and powerful operations and maintenance support.

Base Station Subsystem (BSS)

The base station subsystem, or radio subsystem, provides the distribution function of the radio communication network. It includes Base Transceiver Stations (BTS) which provide the radio link with mobile subscribers.

BTS are controlled by a Base Station Controller (BSC), which can also provide a function of traffic concentration.

BSC controls remote TransCoder Units (TCU) which enables it to reduce the number, and consequently the cost, of PCM (Pulse Code Modulation) links needed between BSS and NSS.

As required by the system, the BSS has a standard interface, so it can be connected to different types of switching centers.

The BSS includes the following features:

Radio engineering assistance:

- frequency hopping (FH),
- discontinuous transmission on voice activity detection (VAD/DTX),
- dynamic power control,
- efficient reception diversity,
- transmission diversity,
- handover on power budget criterion.

Optimization of terrestrial links:

- remote transcoders installed at MSC site,
- BTS control channels multiplexed at site level,
- full multidrop configuration allowed by the BTS.

Network Subsystem (NSS)

The network subsystem handles all switching and routing functions. Mobile-oriented communication networks require a mobile station to be located before a call may be routed and set up.

The Mobile services Switching Center (MSC) is responsible for switching and routing. Reference data, specific to each subscriber, is stored in a database which is distributed among Home Location Registers (HLR).

In order to minimize access to the HLR, the MSC uses a Visitor Location Register (VLR), which contains working data for subscribers moving around its coverage area. Network security and access controls are provided by the Authentication Center (AUC) and by the Equipment Identity Register (EIR).

The distributed architecture of the switching products provide the operator with great flexibility and makes them fulfill the ever changing requirements of an evolving and expanding network with minimum disruption.

Operations Subsystem (OSS)

The operations and support subsystem consists of two distinct parts:

1.   The Radio Operations and Maintenance Center (OMC-R) carries out all usual functions which allow the operator to efficiently manage the digital cellular network he is in charge of.

2.   The Switching Operations and Maintenance Center (OMC-S) offers

wide capabilities in terms of network management (network O&M functionalities may be provided either locally at the MSC or from a specific centralized equipment).

The O&M centers provide the following main features:

- Subsystem configuration and management.
- Performance management, based on collected measurements.
- Fault management, based on alarm and event analysis.
- Security management and monitoring.

Network Internal Services

Call routing and follow-up services are completely transparent to users, but they initiate complex procedures in order to:

- Locate mobile subscribers. Due to its cellular design, the system must be able to locate a mobile station at any time, so calls may be routed to it.

- authenticate mobile subscribers. Each time a procedure, such as call routing or location updating, is initiated between a mobile station and the network, a subscriber's authentication procedure is carried out, in order to prevent fraudulent connections to the network,

- maintain communications. When a call is set up between a mobile subscriber and its called party, the system must maintain the communication, according to the mobile station moves, by means of power control and handover procedures.

Locating

The network must be able to locate any mobile station, so it can route calls to it. Given the cellular design, two types of procedure may be initiated: the location updating and registration procedure and the paging procedure.

Both procedures are simultaneously used to locate the mobile station as precisely as possible.

Cell Selection

Cells are incorporated into geographical groups and their number in a group is determined by the amount of traffic to be handled and by their range. A group of cells is called a location area.

The cellular system requires mobile stations to know which cell they are moving in at any time, so as to be registered by the mobile services switching center (MSC) which controls the location area.

Base transceiver stations (BTS) permanently broadcast general information about their identity on a channel dedicated to that purpose, the BCCH (Broadcast Control CHannel). Mobile stations continuously listen to that channel and know the location area the cell belongs to.

When the mobile station does not handle any communication, the portable terminal is put in a sleeping state for economy purposes. However, it still listens periodically to the BCCH carrier, so as to be ready for receiving a call.

When the mobile station moves from one location area to another, a procedure is initiated between the mobile station and the network which requires the mobile services switching center (MSC), via the base station subsystem (BSS), to update the mobile new position into the visitor database (VLR).

This request leads to executing either a location updating or a registration procedure, depending on which MSC controls the new location area.

If a call is to be routed to the mobile station, the MSC gets its location area from data stored in the VLR. Then, it starts a paging procedure, via the BSS, in all cells that belong to the specified location area. The mobile station picks up the message and starts a call set-up procedure with the MSC via the BSS.

Location Updating / Registration

When a mobile station moves into another cell, it first checks if the new cell belongs to the same location area. If it does, no procedure is initiated. If it does not, the mobile station must register itself to the new location area.

Depending on whether the new location area is controlled by the same MSC or by a different one, a location updating or a registration procedure is carried out.

Both procedures are implemented the same way.

- BTS1 sends a broadcast channel (1) and the mobile station (MS) moves (2),

- BTS2 sends a broadcast channel and MS detects a location area change (3),

- MS makes a random access set-up request to the base station controller (BSC2) which, according to radio resource availability, allocates a signaling channel (SDCCH) to the mobile station,

- BSC2 establishes a connection between the mobile station and the mobile services switching center (MSC2) which controls the new location area,

- MS makes a location updating request to MSC2, via BSC2 and BTS2, by indicating its IMSI (International Mobile Subscriber Identity),

- MSC2 consults its visitor location register (VLR2) for establishing whether the mobile station comes from a location area controlled by itself or a different MSC (4).

If MSC2 controls the former location area, it carries out an authentication procedure (see paragraph entitled "AUTHENTICATION") and, if it is successful, updates the mobile new location data into its visitor database (VLR). This is the end of the location updating procedure.

Otherwise, MSC2 initiates a registration procedure:

- it first asks the HLR for the subscriber's information and authentication data (5) and starts an authentication procedure,

- if it is successful, MSC2 enters the mobile station new location data into VLR2 (6) and informs the HLR that it is not controlling the mobile station (7),

- the HLR stores the identity of the MSC/VLR which now controls the mobile station and informs VLR1 that it can remove all mobile station information from its database (8).

Paging

When a user attempts to call a mobile subscriber, the call is handled by the MSC which controls the location area the mobile station is in and a paging procedure is initiated.

- a call to the fixed network is switched to the mobile services switching center (MSC) (1) which searches its VLR for the location area the mobile station is in (2),
- the MSC sends instructions to the BTS, via one or several BSC, to

page the mobile station in all cells within the location area (3),

■   the BTS send a signal to every cell they control which informs the mobile station that it is called. The mobile station receives the request from BTS2 (4),(5),

■   as soon as the mobile station picks up the message, it carries out a call set-up procedure, as described in paragraph entitled "Mobile terminating calls",

■   when the path is set up, the MSC routes the call to the mobile station.

Authentication

The authentication procedure is designed to prevent the network from unauthorized access. Each time a connection is attempted, the mobile subscriber undergoes an authentication procedure in order to check his IMSI (International Mobile Subscriber Identity). Each IMSI is associated with a secret key (Ki).

This key is stored in the HLR and in a special module inside the mobile terminal, the SIM (Subscriber Identity Module), and is never transmitted on radio waves. The mobile equipment identity number (IMEI) is used to check if the mobile station is not faulty or stolen. In such a case, the attempt to establish a connection is rejected. Confidentiality is also increased by replacing the IMSI with a temporary mobile subscriber identity (TMSI) number which is frequently changed.

The home location register (HLR) hosts an authentication central unit (AUC) which stores the subscriber's IMSI and secret key Ki. Using the IMSI and the secret key, the AUC processes an algorithm which gives out triplets composed of:

●   A random number (RAND)
●   A signed answer (SRES) for signed result
●   A cipher key (Kc)

Upon each HLR request, the AUC generates a certain number of authentication triplets. The HLR sends some of these triplets to the VLR which requests them. One triplet per authentication procedure is used. When its stock is exhausted, the VLR makes a new request to the HLR.

During an authentication procedure, the VLR transmits to the mobile terminal a random number (RAND). The mobile terminal uses this number, together with the secret key (Ki) stored in the SIM, to generate a signed response (SRES) and sends it to the VLR which compares it with the one supplied by the HLR.

sends it to the VLR which compares it with the one supplied by the HLR.

If both are identical, then the connection may be established between the mobile station and the network. If they are not, the connection is immediately rejected.

Communication Supervision

The system is required to maintain a communication with a mobile subscriber when he moves between two cells. The call is maintained by the network, according to the transmission quality and the amount of traffic handled by the cells.

Mobile and base stations permanently carry out radio transmission measurements. Measurements made by the mobile station are sent on a slow signaling channel (SACCH).

The BTS adds its own measurements, analyses them all, and sends the results to the BSC which makes the decision.

Measurements made by the BTS are:

- Reception level
- Reception quality
- Interference level on idle channels
- Distance with MS (TIMING ADVANCE computation)

Measurements made by the mobile station are:

- Reception level
- Reception quality

Two types of procedure may be initiated: the power control procedure and the handover procedure. When transmission quality from MS to BTS falls down, the BSC asks the mobile station to increase transmission power. If transmission by the mobile was already at maximum strength, or if transmission from BTS to MS is considered to be too weak, the BSC proceeds to a communication handover. It also builds an ordered list of the suitable cells.

Traffic handovers are not supported by the BSC. Power control and handover algorithms are carried out, whatever channel is used by the mobile station (traffic channel TCH or dedicated signaling channel SDCCH). However, the BSC does not initialize SDCCH handovers, since such channels have a very short busy period.

When it receives an external handover command, a BSC does not checkout the state of the requested resource, whether TCH or SDCCH.

Power Control

The BSS supports dynamic power control in both directions and static power control in the downlink direction. Power control procedures are carried out by the BSC. The system requires dynamic power control to be performed at MS the level (uplink), while dynamic power control at the BTS level (downlink) is optional.

Dynamic Power Control

Dynamic power control is handled by the BSS in order to optimize both mobile station (MS) and base station (BTS) transmission power. MS and BTS transmission levels are determined by analysis of strength and quality measurements collected in both directions. Power control criteria are set by the operator and processed at the OMC-R.

The more accurate adjustment step is 2 dB or less. Information about call supervision is managed by the BSC in duplex mode.

Static Power Control

The BTS transmission power may be modified on line from the OMC-R by 2 dB steps (or less depending on the manufacturer) within a 12 dB range.

Handover

When a call is in progress, the mobile station measures the quality of the signal received from its cell, as well as from neighboring cells for which the received level is acceptable and on the BCCH of which it was able to synchronize itself and recognize the cell BSIC (Base Station Identity Code). Measurements are sent to the BTS which measures the reception and quality level.

If transmission is at full strength and service quality too low, or if BTS and MS are too far apart, the BSC may decide to carry out a handover procedure, either inside the same cell or with the first cell from a list of preferred order cells suitable to support the call. In the case of a poor uplink transmission (MS-BTS), the BSC may ask the mobile to increase its transmitted power.

The BSS supports both intra-cell and inter-cell handovers. Inter-cell handovers may be either intra-BSC handovers (both cells belong to sites that are controlled by the same BSC) or inter-BSC handovers (each site is controlled by a different BSC which itself may be controlled by a different MSC).
Handovers that occur within a cell or between cells that belong to a same site are

synchronous. Synchronization is provided at site level in the PCS or cellular network.

Handover algorithms play an important role in cellular planning. All parameters (neighboring cell list, maximum power to be used in a cell, maximum distance to a cell, handover margin, power budget in use, level/quality/interference thresholds, average computing laws) are set from the OMC-R. Most of them may be dynamically updated by the operator.

Two types of handover are carried out: the preventive handover (on power budget criteria) and the curative handover (on service quality criteria).

Handover on Power Budget Criteria

The power budget criterion is a powerful mean of restricting a mobile station within an area where the path loss is minimized. Therefore, interference level and transmission power may be minimized too. In an heavy traffic area, most of the handovers should fall into this category.

Handover on Service Quality Criteria

Signal strength and quality, and interference level and BTS-MS distance (call clearing) criteria provide another way of handing over a communication when the power budget criterion cannot be used.

The BSC classifies the cells that will be able to maintain a call, from the best one to the meanest one. When it considers, from information sent by the BTS, that the quality of the call is too low, it starts a handover procedure.

Intra-Cell Handover

The intra-cell handover supported by the BSS is triggered mainly when a channel experiences poor quality. Measurements of interference levels on idle channels are used to select a new channel within the cell.

Intra-cell handovers are given priority over inter-cell handovers within the same MSC. This type of procedure is initiated after the BSC decides to hand over the call to another cell.

The procedure described below relates to a target cell which is controlled by the same BSC.

- A call is in progress between the mobile subscriber (MS) and another user; it is controlled by BTS1.

- The mobile station moves towards another cell.

- The BSC1 decides to hand over the call and allocates a traffic channel (TCH) to the target BTS (BTS2).

- The BSC1 sends the cipher key (Kc), the channel to be used and the frequency hopping sequence to BTS2 and requests the mobile station to connect to BTS2 by sending a handover request to MS via BTS1 which indicates the identity of the target cell.

- The mobile station sends a random access set-up request to BTS2 in order to establish a connection.

- BTS2 informs the BSC1 that the connection has been successfully established and the BSC1 switches the call to the new cell, via BTS2.

- The BSC1 sends a message to the MSC1 which informs it of the transfer and releases BTS1 radio resources.

Depending on where the BTS are located, two cases may arise:

1.   If both BTS are in the same radio location, they use the same time base and the mobile station undergoes a synchronous handover.

2.   If the target BTS is situated in a different radio location, it is not synchronized with the initial BTS: the BSC informs the target BTS that the mobile station must be synchronized and, when the connection is established, the target BTS synchronizes the mobile station by means of the timing advance signal.

Inter-MSC Handovers

The procedure is identical to the one described in "Inter-cell handovers within the same MSC" paragraph, until the initial MSC (MSC1) notices that the target cell is controlled by another MSC.

- MSC1 sends a channel allocation request to MSC2 and indicates the identity of the target cell.

- MSC2 makes a channel allocation request to the BSC3 which controls the target cell (BTS5).

- BSC3 selects and activates radio resources, and informs MSC2.

- MSC2 informs MSC1, which informs BSC2, that the procedure has been carried out.

- BSC2 transmits the handover request to the mobile station, via BTS4.

- The mobile station attempts to connect to BSC3, via BTS5 (see "Inter-cell handovers within the same MSC").

- When the connection is established, MSC1 switches the call to the mobile station, via MSC2, BSC3 and BTS5.

- MSC1 informs BSC2 that it can release all radio resources used,

- MSC2 keeps control of the call and stores all resource information.

When a mobile station, which has already been handed over from MSC1 to MSC2, leaves the area controlled by MSC2, a new handover procedure must be started.

This new procedure is very similar to the one described above and depends on the MSC the new target cell belongs to:

- Either control goes back to MSC1 or;

- Subsequent handover procedure is implemented, which gives control of he call to a third MSC (MSC3).

Updating or a registration procedure follows as required (see "Location updating").

User Services

Some of the services for PCS are yet not fully defined, but it is expected that they will offer similar services to GSM's, as defined for GSM (Global System for Mobile communications). The following services are expected in the following fields.

- Teleservices.
- Supplementary services.
- Bearer services.

The system's modularity should enable the operator to meet user future requirements, by incorporating new service options within existing modules.

Teleservices

Teleservices offered by the system are full end-to-end services, including terminal capabilities, and are designed to meet users' needs in the radio communication field. The following services are expected to be provided:

- Standard telephone services enable mobile subscribers to communicate with other users of telephone networks, whether fixed or mobile.
- Emergency call services enable any mobile or fixed user to call emergency services from the mobile network. These calls take priority over all other calls.
- Short message services enable any mobile or fixed user to send a few tens of bytes long alphanumeric messages to another user.
- Fax group 3 services.
- Other teleservices, such as telex or videotex, will be provided in the future and are only listed in this document. They will be more detailed when introduced by the individual manufacturers.

Telephony

PCS offers great advantages in speech transmission over other analog systems currently in use. Whether sent or received by a mobile subscriber, calls reach a very high speech quality level.

Users of PCS can expect the following features:

- Close to land-line listening quality, whether the mobile station is in motion or halted.
- Solves the problem of radio fading.
- Gets rid of noise on radio waves.
- Greatly reduces interference between two mobile terminals, when they are located close to each other.

Considerable efforts are made to preserve users' privacy. Digitized and ciphered transmission of speech prevents call eavesdropping. Except during call set-up, the IMSI (International Mobile Subscriber Identity) is always transmitted in cipher mode, so that unauthorized people may not locate the mobile station and calls are protected from unwanted listeners.

PCS, which has been hailed by the majority of operators in North America, increases the convenience offered to the traveling subscriber, by ensuring that every call he makes is carried out without being interrupted, as long as he stays within the PLMN (Public Land Mobile Network) corresponding to his subscription area.

Although rates may differ from country to country, it enables a mobile station to send or receive calls, even when outside its home area.

Using a mobile terminal is similar to using a telephone from the fixed network:

■   Dialing of called party numbers is direct and followed by their authentication.

■   Same tones are used, whether it is to inform the user of call routing or when the called party is absent or its line is busy. These signals are usually generated by the mobile telephone itself. Mobile terminal manufacturers are responsible for making these signals sound user friendly.

Two types of call may be established: mobile originating calls and mobile terminating calls.

Mobile Originating Calls

When a subscriber picks up his mobile telephone, a signaling exchange is initiated between the mobile station and the PLMN.

Steps of the call set-up procedure are as follows:

■   The mobile station makes a random access set-up request to the base station controller (BSC), via the BTS.

■   According to radio resource availability, the BSC allocates a signaling channel (SDCCH) to the mobile station.

■   The BSC establishes a connection between the mobile station and the MSC.

■   The mobile station acknowledges the connection and sends a set-up request to the MSC.

■   The MSC carries out a subscriber's authentication procedure (see "Authentication").

■   If the procedure is successful, the MSC requests to switch to cipher mode.

■   The mobile station sends the entire call set-up request to the MSC (subscriber's number, requested service, etc.).

■   The BSC allocates a traffic channel (TCH) and releases the signaling channel (SDCCH).

■   The MSC may then route the call to the fixed network (PSTN) user.

Mobile Terminating Calls

When a user attempts to make a call towards a mobile station, the following procedures are started:

- The PSTN switch, which recognizes the called party's number as a mobile subscriber, routes the call to a specialized server, the GMSC (Gateway Mobile services Switching Center), which starts looking for the mobile station roaming number (MSRN).
- The GMSC sends a roaming number request to the mobile subscriber's home database (HLR: Home Location Register).
- The HLR requests from the mobile subscriber's visitor database (VLR: Visitor Location Register) a specific roaming number to be dedicated to the call.
- The VLR allocates a roaming number and transmits it to the GMSC, via the HLR.
- The GMSC routes the call to the mobile subscriber's host MSC.
- The MSC identifies the subscriber by his roaming number and checks its VLR for the list of cells in which the mobile station should be located.
- The MSC starts a paging procedure towards the areas where the mobile station is supposed to be located (see "Paging"), via base station controllers (BSC) and base transceiver stations (BTS).
- The mobile station is advised that it is searched for and starts a call set-up procedure, as described above.
- The MSC may then route the call to the mobile station.

Emergency Calls

The cellular system offers an emergency call telephone service, available to all subscribers and which enables them to make a call to a centralized emergency service by using a short code or by pressing a single key on the mobile terminal. Calls are routed to the nearest emergency station.

The emergency call set-up procedure is similar to the normal call set-up procedure (see above) and only differs in that the MSC does not carry out the authentication procedure, thus allowing mobile network non-subscribers to make emergency calls from a mobile telephone. The MSC gives first priority to this type of calls.

Short Message Services

The PCS/cellular systems enable users to transmit and receive short messages. These services are implemented by stealing SACCH (Slow Associated Control CHannel) blocks usually reserved for signaling.

They are:

- The mobile terminating / point to point short message service (SMS-MT/PP) for reception by a mobile subscriber.

- The mobile originating / point to point short message service (SMS-MO/PP) for transmission by a mobile subscriber.

- The cell broadcast short message service (SMS-CB) which enables messages of general nature (such as road traffic information) to be broadcast among all subscribers roaming within a given geographical area at regular intervals. As much as 15 short messages can be concatenated to form a macro-message.

Short message services offered to mobile subscribers are better than conventional services offered to alphanumeric pagers, since the mobile station acknowledges reception of the message. Therefore, the system can advise the sender that the message has been received or keep it in case of delivery failure and repeat it as needed. Mobile stations can store the last received messages in a non-volatile memory.

Fax Services

Cellular systems offers a fax service to mobile subscribers in both directions. No definite choice has been made in the technology yet but since PCS has a data interface it is expected to be offered as a service.

Telex Services

Other services specified include telex and vocal message services. They should be made available in the future.

Supplementary Services

When subscribing to the mobile network, users may choose between various services, which add up to the conveniences of basic radio communication services. These services include:

- Calling line identification.
- Call transfer.
- Call barring.
- Call wait, call hold.
- Three-party service.
- Closed user group.
- Charge-related services.
- User-to-user signaling.

Call Line Identification

A mobile subscriber may request to get the number of a party when he tries to call it or when the party tries to call him. He may request his own number not be communicated to a party when he tries to call it or when the party tries to call him. If anonymous or malicious calls are received by a mobile subscriber, he may request the system to give him the calling party's number by pressing a key on his mobile terminal.

Call Transfer

When a call is sent to a mobile station, it may be forwarded to another fixed or mobile network subscriber's number, chosen by the mobile subscriber. When subscribing, the user may ask for this service to be provided and indicates which forwarding number will be used.

This number and the service activation period may be changed by the subscriber at any time.

The system enables a call towards a mobile station to be re-routed once, under the following conditions::

- Unconditionally: whenever the mobile subscriber is unable to receive the call, it is forwarded to a number of his choice.
- If the subscriber's line is busy.
- If the call is not answered.
- If the radio subsystem is congested.,
- If the paging message is not answered.
- If the mobile subscriber is not registered within the searched zone.

■   During the call itself: re-routing may be performed directly from the mobile terminal.

A call transfer, whenever unconditional or due to non-registration, is handled by the HLR. Other call transfers are controlled by the MSC/VLR.

Call Wait / Call Hold

If a call is received by a mobile station while its line is busy, it may be put into a waiting state until the mobile subscriber is ready to take it. Users are warned by a visual or an acoustic signal that a call is waiting. Conversely, the mobile subscriber may put the first party on hold, take the call from the other party and return to the first one later.

Conference Call

A communication service allowing to handle calls between three people when required. This service enables the mobile subscriber to talk to two other users simultaneously. A conference service enables more than three people of the mobile or fixed network to talk to each other simultaneously.

Closed User Group

Subscribers to the mobile network may elect to make a subscription restricted to a group of users. In this case, calls to and from subscribers of the group are limited to the group itself and registration fees are smaller.

Charge-Related Services

Two services are provided:

■   A mobile subscriber may be notified of the amount of charges to be paid for a call (calls to this service are free of charge).
■   A mobile subscriber may call another subscriber who will be charged for the call (call collect).

User-to-User Signaling

This service enables transfer of a limited amount of information between a mobile user and another mobile or ISDN (Integrated Services Digital Network) subscriber during a call, or upon call set-up or release.

For example, it may be used during a call to convey a short message which is visualized on the mobile terminal display or on the ISDN station display.

Call Barring

When subscribing to the mobile network, users may specify call restrictions. It is possible to bar:

- All outgoing calls.
- Outgoing international calls.
- Outgoing international calls, except those towards some countries (for example, all countries members of the European Conference of Postal and Telecommunications Administrations (CEPT)).
- Outgoing international calls, except those towards the home PLMN country.
- Outgoing calls, whenever the mobile station is outside its home PLMN country.
- All incoming calls.
- Incoming calls, whenever the mobile station is outside its home PLMN country.

Bearer Services

These services enable the mobile subscriber to send data in:

- Circuit mode.
- PAD (Packet Assembly/Disassembly) mode.

Circuit mode transmission
This service is used to send data in synchronous or asynchronous duplex circuit mode to the PSTN or the ISDN.

Transmission rate in asynchronous mode may be: 600 bit/s, 1200 bit/s, 1200/75 bit/s, 2400 bit/s, 4800 bit/s, 9600 bit/s.
Transmission rate in synchronous mode may be: 1200 bit/s, 2400 bit/s, 4800 bit/s, 9600 bit/s.

This service enables a mobile station to gain access to a PAD facility in asynchronous mode, at a transmission rate of 600 bit/s, 1200 bit/s, 1200/75 bit/s, 2400 bit/s, 4800 bit/s, or 9600 bit/s.

Packet mode transmission

This service which will be effective in a subsequent version enables a mobile station to send packets of data in synchronous duplex mode, at a transmission rate of 2400 bit/s, 4800 bit/s or 9600 bit/s.

9

Design of the Radio System

An operator has to carry out an extensive radio planning process which should produce radio coverage maps for the whole of the required area. Using digitized maps of the network's terrain, the company determined the exact number and types of cells required, taking into consideration all the necessary parameters, including the environment and any shadowing obstacles.

The next step in the modeling process optimized the frequency range allocated to an operator while minimizing the number of possible interfering sources. Ultimately, these two procedures ensure that each cell has sufficient transmission capacity.

The operator's personnel have to travel extensively around the required area, taking notes and validating regional and local morphologic conditions which could adversely affect the RF propagation signals.

All the input from the field trips has also to be imported into the computer simulation tools used by the company, and the results obtained provide a "true" picture of all environmental conditions present in the target areas.

Radio Coverage Design Parameters

The operator has to set high quality and performance targets for its wireless services in the target areas, comparable to the best networks anywhere in the world.

The company should continue in carrying out extensive testing and fine tuning in order to achieve optimized coverage at all times as well as maintaining a high performing network.

The following are some typical parameters used for radio coverage design requirements.

Parameters	Selected Optimized Values
Minimum acceptable signal level at the mobile	-95 dbm
Minimum acceptable signal levels in coverage zone	-71 dbm Inner City areas (Dense Urban)
	-82 dbm on City roads
	-76 dbm on Urban roads
	-89 dbm on Rural areas
C/I ratio co-channel interference	12 db Urban-Suburban
	12 db rural areas
C/I ratio co-adjacent channel	12 db
Typical Antenna Height above ground	25-28 m Urban and Dense Urban areas
Typical Antenna Height above ground	38 m Suburban-Rural areas
Typical Emitted Radiated Power (ERP)	55 dbm for 18 dbi antennas
	52 dbm for 15dbi Antennas
	48 dbm for omni antennas
Coverage Reliability	90%
Frequency re-use plan	4/12 carrying BCCH

Figure 19: Typical Parameters

Elaboration of the Grid

In order to achieve proper cell location and spacing in each of the different areas, the company must use a grid made of hexagons representing cell coverage.

As the majority of the cells should be sectorized, it means that each cell will be represented by a cluster of three hexagons and that each cluster will be adjacent to each other, forming a grid of equidistant hexagons.

Each different area has a cluster of different sizes, being smaller in Dense Urban areas and larger in Rural areas. The actual size of each cluster has been calculated to optimize the number of possible customers and the coverage parameters as given in the previous table and by the forecast.

Link Budget

The operator has to calculate link budgets based on either GSM recommendations 03.30 for Europe or other appropriate CDMA recommendations for North America, with some adjustments based on practical field experience.

Coverage Reliability

The ability of the MS to communicate with a BTS within an area depends on the radio system to be used and it's coverage reliability. This is a factor to be taken into consideration during the procurement stage of the equipment. This factor is normally defined in terms of contour reliability and area reliability.

Normally, users require a 95% contour reliability while commercial users require 70% contour reliability and 88% area reliability. GSM 3.30, for example, recommends an outdoor coverage of 75% contour reliability and 90% area. The company's network should be designed to comply with this requirement.

Penetration Losses

One of the key objectives is to provide superior coverage for class IV mobiles indoors and in-car mobiles while traveling. The design will take into account penetration loss margins derived from values contained in GSM 03.30, and adapted to suit the operator's field experience, specifically as is related to the dense-urban construction in the target areas.

The following typical values were used in a number of designs:

■   17 db for ground floor penetration of large office buildings in downtown cores.

■   13 db for ground floor penetration of large office buildings in urban areas.

■   9 db for vehicle penetration, including small buildings.

Propagation Modeling

The operator must at least use the modified Okomura-Hata propagation prediction model for calculating the propagation based on the link budgets and antenna heights.

The propagation model is part of a sophisticated set of computer aided radio planning tools, e.g., the PLANET system, Comsearch's and others, which can be used by an operator to predict coverage, channel demand, interference, clutter control, frequency coordination and assignment. The terrain information of the target area must be digitally inputted into the system.

Frequency Allocation and Reuse

In Europe, the cellular spectrum is provided in two bands from 947.5 MHz to 950 MHz and from 955 MHz to 960 MHz corresponding to 38 channels for GSM applications. The author assumes that one half channel will be used as a guard band at each end of each sub-band of the allowed spectrum.

The operators can also use 4/12 re-use patterns implementing an adaptive technique which takes into account the range of different cell sizes. The operator should also take into account any notices of any requirements to co-ordinate frequencies in border areas with other countries.

Surface Clutter Characterization

In order to access the proper behavior and prediction in each of the different attributes, also known as Clutters, they should be characterized individually and tested to assure that the selected optimized values are met in practice.

Therefore the following clutter types can be identified in the target areas and given a proper loss setting.

■   Open Fields.

■   Forests.

■   Water.

■   Dense Urban.

- Urban.
- Sub-Urban.
- Airports.
- Tunnels.

Antennas

As we aim to optimize the frequency re-use plan and to obtain the maximum number of users per cell, each site has been allocated with three sectors, and in order to obtain best coverage patterns, sectorized antennas are normally used in the target areas.

On highways where large coverage is expected and where frequency re-use is less important, Omni-directional antennas should be used. A wide range of brands of antennas already exists in the market and careful selection will result in the operator obtaining the best products and services from the suppliers.

Recently NORTEL announced success with the testing and implementation of their "Smart" antennas. According to NORTEL an improvement of about 50% is noticed in terms of coverage. If the claim is substantiated, then this means that the RF deployment in terms of antennas and real estate would be significantly lower.

This is a development that readers should be keeping an eye on for further announcements since it changes the economies involved in the deployment of a PCS network.

BTS General Presentation

According to the cellular system design, the base transceiver station (BTS) handles the interface function between the fixed network and mobile terminals.

BTS Goals

The BTS provides exchange of radio signaling and speech/data channels between the mobile station (MS) and the network. It handles all radio functions needed for digitized transmission of these channels. It is controlled by a base station controller (BSC).

Furthermore, it is equipped with a fully duplicated switching matrix which provides redundancy capability.

This feature gives the BTS the ability and the flexibility of easily implemented drop and insert techniques without requiring any extra equipment nor specific software. The drop & insert capability enables the number and the length of PCM links needed by the network to be reduced.

Various combinations of radio sites, with star, loop or chain connections, may be used under control of a single BSC.

BTS Location

Each BTS location is determined by the radio coverage needed within a specific area. Due to the system cellular design, the number of BTS depends on parameters such as the location of the area to be covered and traffic to be handled.

In low density areas, BTS must cover wide transmission and reception areas, whereas in high density areas, the number of BTS is greater and each BTS covers a smaller area.

BTS can be configured in order to manage omni or multi-sector (up to 3 sectors). A particular compact and cost-effective option is offered by the designer which enables a tri-sector site to be implemented in a single base cabinet.

The cabinet dimensions, and the fact that no special temperature working conditions are required, make their installation easy and normally make them meet all user requirements quite well.

Mini-BTS type is designed for outdoor and indoor installation, and Standard BTS and Micro-BTS for indoor installation only. In large capacity Standard or Mini BTS, the standard configuration is made of one base cabinet and as many extension cabinets as cells to manage.

BTS Interfaces

A BTS is linked to its controller (BSC) by the Abis interface. Connections with mobile stations use microwave links, by means of the radio interface (or Air interface or Um interface).

The Abis interface connects the BTS to the BSC. Signaling, speech and data channels are transmitted on external PCM links.

The Radio interface transmits signaling and speech/data on air channels between the BTS and mobile stations (MS). Digitized and coded signals are sent:

- Either within the GSM frequency band in Europe (890 to 915 MHz for MS transmission, 935 to 960 MHz for BTS transmission) or;

■   Within the PCS frequency band (1710-1785 MHz for MS
transmission, 1805 to 1880 MHz for BTS transmission).

BTS Functional Architecture

Architecture Principles

The BTS consists of three main parts, each of them dedicated to specific
tasks.

■   The BCF (Base Common Functions) unit provides the interface between
the BTS and its base station controller (BSC). Plus, it handles the
following functions:

1.   Set signaling channel and physical path concentration.
2.   Generate and distribute the system time to all BTS modules.
3.   Supervise and detect all BTS alarms.
4.   Filter some event reports.
5.   Provide local protection of some BTS modules, by implementing
redundant equipment units.

■   The TRX (radio transceiver) units provide all radio and signal processing
functions needed to handle transmission and reception of signaling and
speech/data channels.

■   Antenna coupling units.

Operators may select the hardware configuration of each radio site, according
to ground topology and traffic needs. They may choose between two types:
single-cell sites or multi-cell sites.

Single-Cell Site

A single-cell site consists of a BTS covering a single cell. This BTS includes TRX
(their number depends on the number of radio channels used), a BCF unit and
an antenna coupling unit.

Multi-Cell Site

A multi-cell site enables operators to provide radio coverage for several cells
within a single location. Up to 6 cells per site may be operated. A three-sector
site is the most common configuration.

A multi-cell site includes a greater number of TRX (their number depends on the number of cells and on the number of channels per cell provided), but the BCF unit is common to all cells within the radio site.

BTS Module Components

The three units that compose a BTS include the following sub-modules:

- The antenna coupling units consist of:

1. One reception antenna and if space diversity is used on reception, another antenna.
2. One transmission antenna.
3. One reception multicoupler, and, if space diversity is used on reception, one diversity multi-coupler.
4. Transmission couplers.

- The transceiver units (TRX) consist of:

1. Transmitters (TX)
2. Receivers (RX).
3. TDMA or CDMA frame processors (FP).

- The BCF unit consists of:

1. Up to two synchronization units SYN or SYNO working in active/standby mode, independently of CSW1 and CSW2 units.
2. Up to two control and switching units (CSW) working in active/standby mode (CSWA/CSWB). Each CSW (A or B) consists of one control unit (CSW1) and one switching unit CSW2.
3. Up to four signaling channel concentrator units (DCC).
4. Up to six PCM interface units (DTI).
5. One alarms management unit (ALAT or ALATO).

A radio site may include one or more coupling units, according to the number of transmitters and antennae. The number of multi-couplers depends on whether space diversity is used on reception and on the number of receivers installed on the radio site.

Each receiver (RX) is associated with one frame processor (FP). This module is called FPRX.

One or more transmitters (TX) may be associated to the FPRX module. The BCF unit is unique on a radio site.

Sub-Module Functions

Antenna

In most cases, there will be one transmitter antenna and one receiver antenna (two if space diversity is used) per cell. Selection of the antenna type (radiation diagram, gain, etc.) is left to operators, who will take into account any radio site and coverage specificity.

Reception Multi-Coupler

This unit pre-amplifies the signal received from the reception antenna and distributes it among the various receivers. Add-on extension modules enable signals to be distributed among more receivers.

The reception multi-coupler consists of one splitter per cabinet. The BTS base cabinet is always equipped with a main splitter. The extension cabinets may be equipped with either an extension splitter (single-cell configuration) or a main splitter (multi-cell configuration). All splitters provide outputs to add-on extension cabinets.

For space diversity used on reception, an RX diversity splitter is added on with its own antenna; consequently the reception multicoupler is duplicated and a dual path receiver is used. In case of the Mini-BTS, the diversity function is included in main Rx-Splitter, otherwise a diversity Rx-Splitter is necessary.

Duplexer

The use of a duplexer offers two advantages: It reduces the number of antennas required and improves performance. Two filters in the duplexer enable a single antenna to be used for the transmission and the reception of signals.

With the diversity reception, a duplexer allows only two antennas (instead of three) to be used. It involves a 1 dB-loss.

Transmission Coupler

The transmission coupler concentrates the signals arriving from the transmitters that are destined for a single transmission antenna. It has one or two coupling stages.

Type of coupler available:

1.   Two-way hybrid coupler

It provides high flexibility in frequency management, due to the wide frequency band this type of coupler uses. However, because of insertion losses (3.5 dB) they are intended to be used in low capacity BTS only; It enables the coupling of two TX signals in only one emission signal.

The minimum frequency separation required between TX connected to one hybrid coupler is 200 kHz.

2.   Cavity coupler

A cavity coupler enables the coupling up to TX signals. It can be connected to an extension cavity coupler. The minimum frequency separation required between TX connected to one cavity coupler is 600 kHz.

A cavity coupler is also a duplexer; it has the ability to receive and transmit with the same antenna. The insertion loss is 4.5 dB.

Duplexer

The use of duplexers offers advantages: it reduces the number of antennas and improves performance. Two filters in the duplexer enable a single antenna to be used for transmitting and receiving signals. With diversity reception a duplexer enables the use of two antennas instead of three without a duplexer.

Two-Way Hybrid Coupler

It provides high flexibility in frequency management, due to the wide frequency band this type of coupler uses. It enables the coupling of two TX signals in only one emission signal. The minimum frequency separation required between TX connected to one hybrid coupler is 200 kHz.

Receiver (RX)

Each receiver (RX) operates one TDMA/CDMA frame and handles the following functions:

- Preamplify signal coming from the reception multi-coupler.
- Switch from radio frequency (RF) to an intermediate frequency.
- Filter received signal.
- Digitize the analog signal received from the radio interface.

The receiver (RX) provides the FP with digital samples of the received signal and with the amplification scaling (gain) factor. If space diversity is used, the RX processes two channels and provides the FP with samples and scaling factors for both.

Transmitter (TX)

Use of a transmitter differs, according to the coupling mode:

- In wideband or hybrid coupling mode, one TX operates one TDMA/CDMA frame coming from the associated FP. It only transmits signals for this frame on frequencies defined by the FP.

- In selective or cavity coupling mode, a TX is set to work at a single frequency, the coupler frequency. It permanently scans all FH (Frequency Hopping) bus links coming from the FP. When it detects an indication that data are to be transmitted on its own frequency, it reads and transmits them on its radio channel.

Transmitters handle the following functions:

- GMSK (Gaussian Modulation Shift Keying) modulation. In case of cavity coupling, a GMSK-modulated radio signal is provided by the TX at the input of the appropriate cavity, thus allowing one to tune it to the desired frequency.
- Transposition of signals to be transmitted in the frequency band.
- If hybrid coupling is used, frequency hopping by means of a flexible synthesizer.
- Power amplification, up to a maximum of 25 W (GSM) or 30 W (PCS).
- BCCH (Broadcast Control CHannel) filling, if frequency hopping rules, managed by the FP, do not provide automatic BCCH frequency filling on the radio channel. One specific TX is dedicated to that purpose: it permanently scans the FH bus and checks if the BCCH frequency is transmitted by one of the other TX. If not, it carries out this special frequency itself.

Frame Processor (FP)

A TDMA frame processor consists of a management unit (MNU) and four dual channel processing units (DCU). Each DCU manages two TDMA/CDMA time slots and consists of a signaling processor (SIGN) and two signal processor units (SPU). Each SPU processes one time slot.

For example, NORTEL DCU and SIGN units include INTEL 80186 processors, operating at 16 MHz, with 512 kbytes of read-only memory and 512 kbytes of random-access memory.

The FP processes one TDMA/CDMA frame, i.e., eight time slots. Each time slot may be a common signaling channel (BCCH/CCCH), a dedicated signaling channel (SDCCH/8), or a dedicated traffic channel (TCH).

FP functions include two main parts:

- Communication functions with the BSC.
- Interface functions with mobile terminals.

Communication functions with the BSC are:

- Manage Abis Interface Level 2 and 3 Protocols.
- Route Mobile Terminal and BTS Signaling Towards BSC.
- Set Logical Channels.
- Handle Operations and Maintenance.

Interface functions with mobile terminals are:

- Process Signal and Handle Level 1 Functions.
- Manage Radio Protocol.
- Activate/Deactivate Radio Channels.
- Detect Random Access Requests Carried Out by Mobile Terminals on Broadcast Channels (Bcch) when Establishing Communication.
- Detect Random Access Requests on Traffic Channels (Tch), when Handover Procedures Are Carried Out.
- Transmit Paging Requests, And Repeat These Requests when needed.
- Transmit Quality and Level Measurements on Active Channels (Tch And Sdcch).

Also,

- Compute Measurement Averages and Execute Power Control and Handover, Algorithms.
- Transmit Interference Level Measurements on Idle Channels (Tch and Sdcch).

- Compute Frequency Hopping Rules.
- Equalize and Demodulate Signal Coming from the Rx.
- Estimate and Control Radio Signal Propagation Time (Timing Advance).
- Cipher and Decipher Signal.
- Code and Interleave Data to be Transmitted.
- Separate and Decode Data Received.
- Adjust Radio Coding to E1 PCM Link (A-Law Coding).
- Handle Functions Relating To Discontinuous Transmission (Dtx) and to Voice Activity Detection (Vad) In Both Directions (Uplink and Downlink).
- On One 64 Kbit/s PCM Link Channel (If Remote Transcoders Are Used) Perform Multiplexing of Four 16 Kbit/S Full Rate Radio Channels.
- Mobile Power Management.

Synchronization Unit (SYN or SYNO)

It distributes the time on the GSM TIME bus to BTS equipment units (FPRX and TX). The unit is duplicated for safety reasons exception Micro-BTS. Both units are synchronized on a 4.096 MHz clock signal coming from the CSW unit, which itself is synchronized on the external PCM links.

Management of the time at site level enables one to carry out synchronous handovers between two cells that belong to the same site.

Control and Switching Unit (CSW)

For example, the NORTEL control and switching unit consists of a 16 MHz INTEL 80186 microprocessor, with 256 kbyte of read-only memory and 256 kbyte of random-access memory. Both memory chips may handle up to 512 kbyte.

The CSW unit includes two modules: the management unit CSW1 and the non-blocking switching matrix CSW2, which handles 16 V11 internal PCM links. Most manufacturers tend to use a similar memory configuration.

Data Channel Concentrator Unit (DCC)

A typical DCC unit consists of a 16 MHz INTEL 80186 or equivalent microprocessor, with 256 kbytes of read-only memory and 256 kbytes of random-access memory. Both memory chips may handle up to 512 kbytes. The DCC unit is controlled by the CSW via the O&M bus.

This unit concentrates up to four signaling channels sent by the FP on a single time slot at 64 kbit/s via the internal PCM links. This time slot is sent back to CSW2, which switches it towards the BSC via the DTI unit on an external PCM link vice versa.

Each DCC unit may manage 15 channels (for example, 12 coming-in channels are concentrated on 3 going-out channels). Three DCC units are needed to concentrate signaling channels coming from the 24 FP and secondary signaling channels coming from other units.

In a two-sector or a three-sector site, one DCC unit per cell is used. The standard BTS may be fitted with a maximum of four DCC units, one of which is reserved for redundancy use. Typically a Mini-BTS may be fitted with a maximum of two DCC units.

Digital Trunk Interface Unit (DTI)

As an example a NORTEL unit will be used which consists of a 68HC11 MOTOROLA controller, with 40 kbytes of read-only memory and 16 kbytes of random-access memory. It is controlled by the CSW via the O&M bus and provides interface and synchronization of the external PCM links upon transmission and reception.

One unit manages one external PCM link. The BTS may be fitted with six (Standard BTS) or two (Micro or Mini-BTS) units.

10

Design of the Switching System

Digital Switch Architecture

A typical digital switch is composed of a number of building blocks, each with its own internal architecture. Digital switches utilize SPC (Stored Program Control) and time division multiplexing (TDM) for the high speed switching of Pulse Code Modulation (PCM) signals.

Digital facilities (Typically DS-1) are interfaced directly and multiplexed into a high speed digital bit stream for processing and transmission across the switch. Combining the transmission with the switching medium provides an integrated transmission path which maintains PCS carrier transmission quality.
These techniques result in compact, highly reliable, large traffic capacity digital switch systems with virtually non-blocking characteristics.

Digital switches use hardware and software modularity to facilitate extensions and additions of new features and enhancements. The central control is relieved of some critical real time functions by using peripheral processors to perform simple repetitive tasks. This distribution of processing also simplifies the software structure of the main program.

The digital switch has been developed (manufacturer dependent) with appropriate software and hardware options for Class 1 to Class 5 operations. Its architecture can typically be sectionalized into three major functions:

- Central Control
- Switching Network
- Peripherals

Central Control Processing

The central control is a computer system that controls operation and maintenance of the digital switch. The system contains high speed central processor units, memory store, peripheral controllers, and a high speed address and control bus system.

The memory store is typically divided into two basic memory types: program store and data store. Program store contains software required for call processing and OA&M functions, while data store contains office dependent data such as customer information and transient call information.

Controllers are used to interface the CPU to the switch's peripherals and its switching network. They allow the CPU to sense the status of the system and to control the telephony switching equipment. The AC bus system provides a means of communicating between the CPUs, memory stores, and peripheral controllers.

There are primarily three types of central control: parallel synchronous, triplex synchronous, and load sharing. Parallel synchronous architecture consists of two CPUs each having dedicated instruction and data store memories that are accessed over separate buses. Both CPUs and their associated memory normally operate in synchronism and process the same information; however, only the designated active CPU will control any outputs.

Triplex synchronous architecture consists of three CPUs which are connected to two duplicated sets of processor buses with no more than two CPU's appearing on any bus. Load Sharing architecture consists of CPU's operating in asynchronous mode. Both CPU's operate alternately in a "load sharing" mode; however, the processing of an individual call is assigned to a specific CPU.

Network

The switching network provides for the interconnection of incoming and outgoing circuits. It accomplishes this using instructions from the central control.

A switching network may be designed to operate with a folded or unfolded architecture. The folded network has all incoming and outgoing network appearances combined on one side of the STS matrices, whereas the unfolded network has separate incoming and outgoing appearances.

Since the folded network has all appearances one side, it reduces the number of trunk circuits required and results in more efficient wiring arrangements.

The modularity of the switching network permits orderly growth from the minimum number of terminations to the maximum capacity of the switch.

Network reliability may be improved by implementing a duplicated switching network or redundant segments.

Peripherals

The digital switch utilizes the peripheral sub-systems to access the outside world as shown in the following graphic.   They provide functions such as synchronization, timing, speed, and format conversion between facilities (analog or digital) and the internal structure of the digital switch.   The actual peripheral design varies with each switch manufacturer and may take the form of an individual peripheral module for each specific application or a peripheral encompassing several functions.

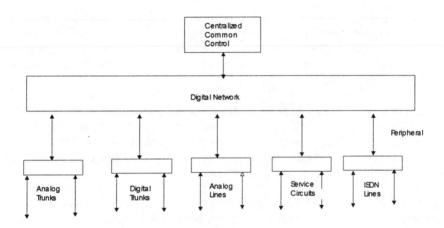

Figure 20: Digital Switch Architecture

Operational Interfaces

Although peripheral units provide the digital switch with access to the outside world, there also remains the requirement for a free flow of information between the switch and the operating personnel. Various input/output ports are provided on the switch for this purpose and can be classified as man/machine interfaces (MMI).

Maintenance and Administration Interface

The assignment of the maintenance and administration interfaces varies among organizations. Functions may be combined or kept separate in accordance with each organizations individual requirements.

Data Interfaces

Most digital switches are capable of exchanging various types of information with terminals located in remote locations. Currently, low speed data interfaces and interfaces for packetized transferal of bulk data are provided.
Common Channel Signaling (CCS see following sections) interfaces are being developed (optimized) for high speed data exchange.

Software

Digital switch software is designed to operate in a "real time" environment to efficiently handle call processing as well as OAM&P functionality. It must be flexible to cater to office growth and new service features. Software system functions can be categorized as administrative, call processing, maintenance and control.

Administrative functions include system loading and initialization, system fault analysis, traffic data collection, software audits, and various other support functions. Call Processing (CP) functions include trunk and line scan, call sequence control, digit analysis and translation, network control and management, and billing data accumulation.

Maintenance functions   include fault detection, fault recovery, system diagnostics, alarm supervision, and support of various manual and automatic test functions.

Control functions include processor task allocation, transfer of information within the system, and allocation of system resources.

The system software comprises office dependent software and generic software. The office dependent software varies with site and mode of operation. The generic software is common to all sites.

Software Maintenance

The digital switch relies upon the integrity of its resident software system for the correct processing of calls. However, because of the size and complexity of digital switch software programs, it is virtually impossible to produce a system load program which is error free.

Thus the software system of a digital switch requires maintenance to ensure that functional problems are identified on an ongoing basis and program changes are implemented for their changes.

Problem identification is accomplished by hardware and software mechanisms continually verifying the software integrity through such means as out-of-range checks on data table lengths, timers to guard against software loop errors, and software organization audits to confirm that software processes are being executed correctly.

Except for extremely urgent corrections, the errors in program modules are accumulated, and changes are made in the system software on a scheduled basis. Because changes are a potential source of new program errors, it is often desirable to maximize the interval between successive program reloads in order to ensure thorough debugging of the resident load.

For more urgent corrections, software changes are facilitated through the use of "Patching" techniques. This allows for small changes in base software code during the regular operation of the CPU without a full recompile of the existing program. Software maintenance is generally required for the lifetime of a digital switch.

System Design Objectives and Concepts

High Service Quality

Three items are required for service quality:

1.   **Coverage**: The system should serve an area as large as possible. With radio coverage, however, because of irregular terrain configurations, it is usually not practical to cover 100 percent of the area for two reasons:

- The transmitted power would have to be very high to illuminate weak spots with sufficient reception, a significant added cost factor.

- The higher the transmitted power, the harder it becomes to control interference

2.   **Required Grade of Service**: For a normal start-up system the grade of service is specified for a blocking probability of .02 for initiating calls at busy hours. This is an average value. However, the blocking probability at each cell site will be different. At the busy hours, near freeways, automobile traffic is usually heavy, so the blocking probability at certain cell sites may be higher than 2 percent, especially when car accidents occur. To decrease the blocking probability requires a good system plan and a sufficient number of radio channels.

3.   **Number of Dropped Calls**: During Q calls in an hour, if a call is dropped and Q-1 calls are completed, then the call drop rate is 1/Q. This drop rate must be kept low. A high drop rate could be caused by

either coverage problems or handoff problems related to inadequate channel availability.

System Compatibility: Design the system to be fully compatible to technology standards (i.e., GSM, etc.). This will limit problems encountered due to interconnect or technology issues.

Systematic Expansion: System design should utilize "scaleable" components which allow for effective system evolution and transition.

Voice Quality: Voice quality tends to be difficult to judge without subjective tests from user's opinions. For any given commercial communications system, the voice quality should be based on the following criterion: a set value of x which y percent of customers rate the system voice quality (from transmitter to receiver) as good or excellent.

Factors Impacting System Design

The following five factors impact the system design.

1.   Terrain conditions i.e., flat, hilly, etc.
2.   Density of subscribers.
3.   Anticipated volume of traffic generated by each subscriber.
4.   The established network (if any), its capability for extension, its suitability for the support of any new services, its state of repair, and its degree of obsolescence.
5.   The reliability, optimum size, and service capabilities of contemporary equipment which might be used to extend or replace the established network.

Design Considerations

The chosen switching platform must be designed to meet the projected growth rate of the system. The capability of the switch to provide reliable uninterrupted service with a large MTBF is also a design consideration.

Operational Reliability

The digital switch makes extensive use of distributed processing, and duplication of critical common equipment such as the CPU memory, peripheral controllers and message controllers. Diagnostic programs ensure that the high reliability requirements of the switch are met by performing self-diagnostics on the operational and call processing functions as well as hardware.

Duplication typically includes the use of separate busing and power feeds for each individual unit of equipment pairs so that the occurrence of a single fault will limit the impact on the overall switching system.

Software diagnostic programs continuously monitor the operational status of the switch with respect to hardware and software integrity, and on detection of a fault, will perform corrective action to isolate the detected fault.

Under most fault conditions, the digital switch is capable of maintaining call processing at normal or near normal capacity. A combination of faults, such as the failure of both CPUs, will cause the system to go out of service. The probability of this scenario occurring is extremely minimal.

Operational Systems

The successful operation of a digital switch is dependent on the functionality of various internal and external test facilities, diagnostic tools, and maintenance aids. Each developed capability is enhanced or built on to develop further capabilities until the entire system is operational. This allows the system to virtually test itself.

Test Systems

Numerous test systems are required for the maintenance of analog and digital facilities attached to a digital switch. These test systems should be accessible via the switch's man/machine interface (MAP, MTP, etc.) using internal or external test equipment attached through the switch network at a suitable test access point.

Transmission Considerations

The digital switch has considerable impact upon network transmission, both in terms of the transmission equipment control functions that the switch must provide and the impact that its own design has upon transmission performance. In terms of control, the digital switch must control the application of digital pads depending the type of transmission facility utilized.

Echo control devices may be integrated within the digital switch; however, stand-alone echo control is more common. Internal or external echo cancellation will require control accordingly. In terms of switch design, the digital switch has an impact on delay, error and other performance related characteristics of the digital signals transmitted through its network.

Echo Control

Because of the technology used in digital PCS applications, echo control and cancellation is an important function which needs to occur in the switching and transmission environment.

Network Synchronization

Digital communications is highly dependent on the accurate timing alignment of the digital signal. This dependence on precise timing is one of the main differences between analog and digital communications.

Accurate timing is necessary in time division multiplexing (TDM) to interleave each byte or each bit into its appropriate time slot. Demultiplexers must operate in step with digital signal frame timing to extract each 8 bit word. Similar coordination is required in digital switches.

In order to attain frame synchronization, all digital nodes and transmission facilities must be controlled by clocks of the same frequency. That is, all network clocks must be synchronized. Network synchronization is achieved by locking the frequency of all nodal clocks to a primary frequency source.

Maintaining network synchronization depends on the accuracy with which the clock at each node can lock onto the primary frequency source, the minimization of transmission variations which may upset the distribution of the synchronizing information, and the accuracy of local clocks when a synchronizing link fails.

Synchronization Methods

There are two common methods for nodal synchronization plesiochronous and mesochronous. Plesiochronous architecture uses local clocking running independently with periodic manual adjustment to maintain alignment. Mesochronous synchronization uses nodal clocks locked on to an external reference link to provide node synchronization.

Timing Reference Distribution

The standard reference frequency must be distributed to all switching nodes for network synchronization. Typically, DS-1 signals are used as reference links to convey network timing.

- TOD synchronization between time zones.
- Multiple time zones supported by one switch.

Physical Characteristics

Power Requirements

The digital switch's power demands are relatively insensitive to variations in traffic load, particularly where analog interfaces to the switch are few in number. A centralized type of power fusing and distribution system is generally used with digital switches.

The purpose of the power distribution system is to provide adequately controlled and protective distribution of DC power (nominal -48 volts office battery) and AC power (115 volts 60 Hz in North America, and 220 volts 50 Hz in Europe) for the switching office.

The AC and DC power distribution systems are completely separated with the exception of some common grounding arrangements.

AC provides the supply for normal office lighting and convenience outlets. Any requirements (such as cooling fans) for protected AC is provided by inverters fed from the office DC supply, with commercial AC as backup.

The distribution and fusing of DC power to the switch is such that no more than fifty percent of any given type of equipment will be supplied from one fuse. In the event of a commercial power failure, the office DC battery requires sufficient reserve to provide uninterrupted power to the switch for a pre-determined period.

The reserve time/battery capacity decision is dependent upon the size and class of office and also on the AC power backup configuration.

The central office and switching equipment grounding system is designed to provide adequate protection and isolation to personnel and equipment from foreign potentials. It also ensures proper system operation by minimizing the effect of any electrical noise.

Environmental Considerations

High density packaging, particularly of such items as line, trunk and service circuits, gives rise to associated problems of heat dissipation. Also, electronic components are designed to operate within certain temperature and humidity tolerances.

Hence, environmental controls are generally required to ensure system reliability. Because of this, heating, air conditioning, and humidity control systems are mandatory for digital switch offices.

The digital switch and ancillary equipment are designed for normal operation under specific ambient changes within designated temperature and humidity limits and also for extended intervals (dependent upon switch manufacturer) under extremes of environmental limits.

Hardware Considerations

The digital switch is typically configured on a modular basis with extensive use of plug-in units which allows for the orderly and progressive growth of the switch from minimum to maximum capacity without major rearrangement of equipment.

The requirement for different types of printed circuit boards, mounting shelves, and equipment frames are minimized through standardization. Additionally, all inter-frame cabling is pre-formed and inter-connectable.

The modular approach allows for a relatively short installation time. The addition of plug-in units provides for the most extension; frame hardware additions are required occasionally. This results in faster reaction to unexpected forecast increases and a shorter provisioning interval.

Floor Space

The degree of component integration and modularity of digital switching components allows for highly reduced floor space requirements (relative to older analog and digital switches) and flexibility in the arrangement of equipment frames, excepting certain critical cable length restrictions (technology dependent).

In general, the equipment should be grouped:

1.   To eliminate cable routing congestion.
2.   To minimize total cable runs and cross sections.
3.   To facilitate administrative and maintenance functions.
4.   To allow for orderly growth for future extensions.
5.   To satisfy building floor loading requirements.
6.   To satisfy heat dissipation requirements.

The location of distribution frames and power distribution systems will also influence the digital switch equipment layout.

Switching Hierarchy

The nationwide telephone network in the past has been comprised primarily of one company operating in each geographic area with each such company interconnecting with other companies serving other areas according to a well standardized hierarchy of interconnections.

In recent years, the advent of numerous competing interconnect and cellular companies in the same geographical area providing long distance services via their own routes and interconnecting with the local telephone networks at many different points has caused the structure of the total telephone system to become more complex. The present day system is still based on a standard hierarchy as displayed in Figure 18 on the next page.

Access to local subscribers in the Exchange Area Network (EAN) is provided by the Class 5 or Central Office (End Office). The area covered by a Central Office (CO) may range from a few square kilometers in a dense urban area to a few hundred square kilometers in a rural area. Also part of the EAN are the Toll Centers (TC), Primary Centers, and Sectional Centers.

These are all interconnected with other similar exchanges at the same level and at the next-higher and the next-lower levels. Each such EAN is connected to one or more Regional Centers as well as having interconnections at various levels with the adjoining EAN.

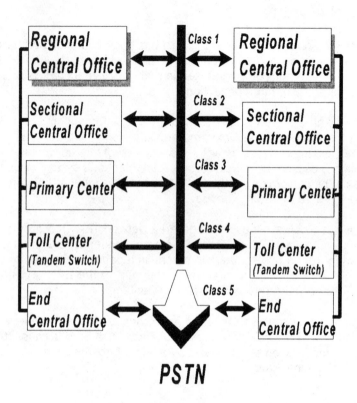

Figure 21: Telephone Network Switching Hierarchy

Conclusion

The PCS switching hierarchy will initially be implemented in a non-hierarchical or fully distributed architecture. In this form, almost all switches will act as a class 5 (end office) as well as a tandem switch for inter-switch, long distance, and PSTN routes.

Significant growth of the operator's PCS network may require the addition of standalone tandem switches to optimize connectivity for long distance into the PSTN as well as other IEC service providers.

Switching Technical Plans

Routing Plan

To maintain high transmission quality and to ensure the minimization of time delays and network costs both on call set-up and on message or speech propagation, it is desirable to minimize the overall number of links and exchanges making up a connection. Routing is an integral part of switching and call processing.

The switching network will need to determine the actual route the call will use based on a number of different parameters including:

1.   Dialed digits.
2.   Originating subscriber's location.
3.   Terminating subscriber's location.
4.   Time of day.
5.   Existing infrastructure.

Routing is implemented and optimized to meet the following network objectives:

■   Selection of an economical routing path conforming with transmission plan requirements.
■   Minimize the likelihood of rapidly escalated network congestion and to minimize the probability of blocking.
■   The need to charge for calls in line with the incurred costs as well as the need to maximize use of owned vs. leased facilities. Note that the cost of a specific call to a subscriber is set by the applicable tariff and is not affected by choice of routes. The cost that is being minimized is the cost to the service provider.
■   Minimize the overall number of links in a connection.
■   Development of a policy of preferred transmission media (if the option exists).
■   The need to avoid circular routings.

Routing Considerations

In large multi-office cities, direct trunks will be provided from each local office to every other local office where there is sufficient traffic to economically justify them, or geographic requirements need to be met (i.e., inter-MSC hand-off). Also, each local office generally has trunks to and from one or more tandem switching systems.

Calls between offices not directly connected are completed through a tandem switching system. Since every local office is connected to a tandem, the tandem network may also be used to provide an alternate route for each of the direct groups. In that case, fewer direct trunks would be needed.

Furthermore, with the ability to alternate-route through a tandem, it generally becomes economical to accommodate growth by establishing new direct groups of small size between offices not previously served by direct groups and thus reduce requirements for tandem switching.

Because alternate routing can be done automatically, it is used extensively to provide economies and service advantages. Calls can be offered in succession to a series of alternate routes via one or more tandem centers. In an emergency situation of limited impact and extent, the ability to use an alternate route provides a measure of protection to service.

However, if there is a heavy surge of traffic over an entire area (as in a major disaster such as a hurricane), there is little margin to absorb such surges in load, and the service cannot be as good as it would be with a non-alternate-route network.

The principle of alternate routing is basic on the design of the network. Switching equipment automatically seeks out the alternate routes. At each switching system, all of the high usage trunk groups to which a call can be offered are kept busy with a portion of the traffic overflowing to other routes. There are fewer final trunk groups, and the engineered level of service is good. The overall chance of completing a call is improved by the fact that it can be offered to more than one trunk group.

The switching equipment operates rapidly and there is no significant change in speed of service between the selection of direct and alternate routes.

In addition to the final trunk groups that connect switching systems to their home switching centers, HU (high usage) trunk groups to other switching systems subject to the rules of the network hierarchy are provided wherever it is economical to do so.

However, there are no direct routes for calls to many low-volume points. The first route for such calls is a switched route over two or more trunk groups of the network in tandem in accordance with the standard routing pattern.

Routing Rules Overview

For traffic to be carried efficiently over a distributed or hierarchical network, it is necessary to have standard rules for routing that traffic. The rules summarized below have two applications.

They supply the foundation for the routing discipline which provides the logic for accumulating loads for the purpose of identifying trunk group candidates, and they specify how traffic should be routed in a network in which trunk groups and homing arrangements are known.

Adherence to the rules in the network expansion process will provide for orderly network growth and permit achieving the objectives of standardized routing and carrying traffic at lower levels in the network on the fewest practicable links.

Routing traffic on an existing network in accordance with the same rules will ensure that calls have access to those trunk groups where capacity has been provided for them.

The following rules will satisfy most network requirements. However, local situations may justify deviation from these rules.

There are 11 basic rules that govern the selection of first routes and alternate routes in the network design process. Note that this document will only provide a summary of the routing rules.   Specific details can be obtained from BellCore documentation SR-TAP-000191.

1.   **Two-ladder Limit**: Traffic must route only via the routing ladders of the originating and terminating switching systems.

2.   **Two-Ladder Direction**: Switched traffic must only route toward the terminating location upward in direction on the originating ladder, and downward on the terminating ladder

3.   **Multiple Switching Function**: A switching system performing multiple switching functions must be assumed to have a routing ladder internal to the switching system extending from its lowest function to its highest function.

4.   **One Level Limit Rule**: When evaluating potential candidate trunk groups, consider only those first-route traffic items for which the switching functions performed at each end of the trunk group differ by no more than one level.

5.   **Switch Low Rule**: Switched traffic must route via tandems involving the lowest level of switching, considering both routing ladders.

6.   **Traffic Grouping Rule**: If there is a choice of routes involving switching at the same level in each of two routing ladders, the route using that functional level I with the terminating ladder should be chosen.

7.   **Single Route Rule**: Routes must be chosen so there is only one

first-choice route from one switching system to another regardless of the switching functions performed by those switching system.

8.   **Load Accumulation Sequence Rule**: In the evaluation of potential candidate high-usage trunk groups at each level in the routing ladder, loads must be accumulated in the following sequence:

Two-way loads between equal switching functions in different ladders.

One-way loads from that base switching function in one ladder to the next higher switching function in the distant ladder, plus two-way loads between the base switching functions of the two terminals of the trunk group being evaluated.

Two way loads between the base switching function in one ladder and the base plus next high switching function in the distant ladder.

9.   **Two-Way Interdependency Rule**: New trunk group candidates produced by the summation of two-way loads between a switching function and the next higher switching function may be interdependent due to a " duplicate routing" of some traffic items.

When some of these trunk group candidates fail to meet the minimum load criteria after removing the duplication, those to be retained must be determined in accordance with the following priorities:

■   Trunk groups in previous planning.
■   Trunk groups terminated at tandem of lowest class.
■   Trunk groups with highest load.

10.   **Alternate Route Selection Rule**: The alternate route selection at each end of a high usage trunk group must be the route the traffic item between the terminals would follow if the HU trunk group did not exist.

11.   **One Switch Alternate Route Rule**: In identifying potential trunk group candidates, the alternate route at either end of a HU trunk group must consist of no more than two trunk groups with one intermediate switch.

Conclusion

The above discussed routing concepts generally refer to a developed hierarchical switching network and as such may not be applicable to the operator's PCS network. It is assumed that, in its early years, the network architecture will follow a distributed configuration, with numerous access path to PSTN interconnects.

However, long term growth and expansion will require routing plans which must follow many of the standard rules defined above.

Traffic Engineering Considerations

Trunk Group Measurements

The following paragraphs provide a general overview of trunk group data, including a general description of their source and purpose. The various types of trunk group measurements and their data preferences are also discussed. General guidelines for planning a trunk group data program that includes trunk group data administration, scheduling, and processing are also included.

Trunk group data are measurements of the traffic on a group of trunks. Trunk group data are sometimes expressed as either a count of events (peg count) or as a carried load (usage) during a given time interval. Time intervals are normally 1 hour of data.

Uses of Trunk Group Data

Adequate amounts of accurate trunk group data are essential to users of the data. Users are the following:

- The network planner, who needs trunk group data to plan, design, maintain, and revise trunking layouts and switching systems which will provide trunking networks that are both service oriented and cost efficient.
- The trunk service person (traffic engineer) , who needs trunk group data that accurately reflect the most recent condition of the network so that decisions can be made about adding/disconnecting trunks.
- The trunk forecaster, who needs trunk group data to develop base data for projecting future trunk requirements and supporting special network studies.
- Network administration and support groups, who need trunk group data for network monitoring and reporting purposes.
- Other users, who need trunk group data for purposes such as corporate statistics and marketing studies.

Types and Sources of Trunk Group Measurements

Traffic measurement devices and mechanized systems are essential tools for the trunk engineer. They provide the data necessary to design and maintain trunking layouts which will provide the quality of service that meets service objectives. But, if provision and use of the devices and systems are not adequate, or if their operation is faulty, the effect can be significant from the standpoint of future serve and costs.

The trunk engineer is obligated to take a firm stand on adequate measurement facilities as well as on the quality of maintenance required to ensure accurate and dependable operation of those facilities. In addition, adequate arrangements must exist for the processing of these measurements so that the resulting data can be used to the best advantage.

There are several types of trunk group measurements that fall into one of two categories:

- Load Oriented. Data counts or measurements that are indicative of the load carried or offered to a trunk group.

- Congestion Oriented. Data counts or measurements that are observed only when congestion on the trunk group is evident.

The principal load-oriented indicators used are:

- Usage (U). A measurement of either the observed load carried or occupied time of a trunk or a group of trunks. Usage is usually expressed in CCS for ease of calculation.

- Peg Count (PC). A measurement of the number of attempts made to seize any outgoing trunk in a group. PC is frequently referred to as the number of calls offered.

The principal congestion-oriented indicator is Overflow (O). Overflow is a measurement of the number of calls or attempts failing to find an idle trunk. Overflow is usually expressed as percent overflow, which is a calculation derived from measurements and describes the percent of the offered load failing to find an idle trunk. Percent overflow is the ratio of attempt failures to the total attempts times 100, where O/PC= percent overflow.

A suggested measurement preference is as follows:

1. Usage, peg count, and overflow is the first choice for all categories of trunks.
2. Usage only is the second choice if usage, peg count, and overflow are unavailable.

3.   Peg count and overflow is the third choice if usage is unavailable.
4.   Peg count only is the fourth choice.
5.   Overflow only is the fifth choice.

Note: Preferences 3, 4, and 5 are not recommended for use in engineering a trunk network because of the less accurate estimate of offered loads generated by their use.

Considerations for a Trunk Group Data Program

A comprehensive trunk group data program can be effective only when certain items that go into the program have been carefully considered.

Some of these items are:

•   Methods of collecting data. The data collection methods used should be the most cost/service effective available for the types of installed and planned switching system equipment.

•   Turnaround time. Trunk group data, to be usable, must be accurate and current. The traffic engineer can react to network congestion only when there is an awareness of the problem when it exists.

Trunk group data must be accumulated, validated, and processed. Trunk group data received within 3 weeks may be considered current. Turnaround time greater than 4 weeks from the measurement period should be investigated and the reasons for delay corrected.

•   Collection Intervals. Sound traffic engineering decisions for network planning, forecasting, and servicing are made based on trunk group data received during significant hours. The trunking data collection intervals should include the three possible major busy seasons (each consisting of 20 consecutive average business days.).

This busy season data collection is a minimum trunk group data collection requirement. However, by using computerized collection systems, much more than the minimum trunk group data collection requirements can be obtained.

While traffic engineers rely heavily on current trunk group data for network planning and forecasting purposes, they also use historical data to validate current data, estimate missing data, and build historical data files. It is imperative to retain historical data files for all in-service and discontinued trunk groups.

Retrial Effects on Offered Load Calculations

The following discussion examines the impact on trunk group measurements due to customer and/or operator retrials when No Circuit (NC) conditions are encountered. Accounting for retrials can result in substantial trunk savings on some trunk groups.

Interpreting Trunk Data Affected by NC

A matter of major importance in the engineering and administration of all grade-of-service trunk groups is the interpretation of Usage (U) readings when NC conditions exceed planned levels. At such times, there is an increase in repeated attempts.

Some attempts result in calls which are completed, and, hence, are included in carried load measurements. Other attempts remain in the blocked category and are abandoned; that is, subsequent attempts are not completed within the hour initially offered, and often not with the same day.

Overall Effects of Retrials

Trunking theories that relate offered loads and expected percentage of overflow traffic (when it has no alternate route) assume that blocked calls are immediately abandoned and do not return within the period of measurement (usually one hour). Immediate abandonment is true in many instances.

However, a substantial proportion of the blocked calls are commonly repeated one or more times at the discretion of the calling customers.

The overall effect of customer and operator retrials on uncompleted calls must, when the blocking is 5 percent or more and the group has seven or more trunks, be taken into account in determining the first attempt offered load and in the corresponding provisioning of trunks.

Corrections of measured loads for retrial assume significance and are suggested at NC values of 5 percent or more, but not for groups with six or less trunks. At lower blocking levels, and in groups with six or less trunks, the adjustment has negligible effect and is not deemed to be needed.

Extensive formulae and derivations exist to account for adjusting measured loads to account for retrials; however, these will not be discussed in this book.

Sizing the Network

General

This section will summarize procedures to convert trunk group measurements into estimates of average offered loads, as well as to convert average offered loads into trunk requirements. These conversion procedures provide the necessary adjustments for the effects of day-to-day and within-the-hour variations of offered and overflow loads.

Sizing Concepts

The sizing concepts described below are a series of operations that deal with the conversion of trunk group load and service measurements to average offered and first-route loads, and average offered loads to trunk requirements in an existing network.

All manual procedures covered use average load and service measurements. The averaged data consists of a minimum of five days and a maximum of twenty days. The user is cautioned that the minimal number of days will result in a database that is too small to be statistically sound.

Listed below are all the load and service measurements that are required in these procedures, along with a description of how each is derived.

It is imperative that all data used in a particular procedure be from the same study period and from the same time-consistent hour.

Average Offered Load **a**

The average offered load is calculated by averaging the time consistent hourly offered loads:

$$a = \frac{1}{n}\sum_{1}^{n}\left\{\frac{Li}{1 - \dfrac{Oi}{PCi}}\right\}$$

Where Li   = hourly carried load
Oi   = hourly overflow
Pci   = hourly peg count
n   = number of days of data

1.   Average Carried Load Lav: The average carried load is computed from hourly carried loads for a time-consistent hour by totaling the hourly carried load in CCS and dividing by the number of days for that hour in the study period .

2.   Average Peg Count PCav: The average peg count is computed by totaling the hourly peg count registrations for each time consistent hour during the study period and dividing by the number of days in the study period.

3.   Average overflow calls Oav: Computed by totaling the hourly overflow registrations for each time-consistent hour during the study period and dividing by the number of days in the study period.

4.   Average Blocking ratio bav: Computed by dividing the hourly overflow registration each day by the corresponding hourly peg-count registration.

5.   The average blocking ration for each time-consistent hour is then computed by summing the hourly blocking ratios and dividing the total by the number of days in the study period.

6.   Average Holding Time Htav: Ccomputed either by special studies or by utilizing usage, peg count and overflow data. The development of the HTav from UPCO data (Usage, Peg Count, and Overflow) is identical for all types of trunk groups and consists of dividing the average carried load (Lav) in CCS times 100 by the quantity (average peg count minus the average overflow).

$$HTav = \frac{Lav}{PCav - Oav} *100$$

The value of the HTav so derived is an average holding time, in seconds, for all calls carried. It is assumed that the holding time of calls carried is equal to the holding time of all calls offered to the trunk group.

Procedures for Sizing Trunk Groups

The specific procedures for sizing trunk groups will not be defined specifically in this document. Step by step procedures for determining trunk group sizing can be further researched by reviewing the flow charts provided in BellCore documentation SR-TAP-000191.

Conclusion

Traffic engineering will play a key role in ensuring efficient and cost effective trunking between the operator's switching network and all other interconnect networks. The concepts listed above merely touch the surface of the traffic engineering challenges which will ultimately present themselves as the operator's PCS network evolves and expands across a country.

Effective traffic planning and engineering will optimize interconnect costs, and provide a grade of service which will be indicative of the high quality network which an operator will implement.

Signaling

Overview

Signaling includes a variety of addressing, control, and supervisory functions which are necessary for establishing connections through the switched network. These include address information for call routing, controls to initiate circuit seizure and release, and supervision for indications such as answer signal and call disconnect.

Traditional signaling systems typically fall under DC (direct current) or AC (alternating current) signaling. However, more recent signaling methods have evolved to satisfy the large bandwidth requirements inherent in the evolving integrated digital networks.

The functions of a signaling system may be divided into three main categories:

1.   Supervision.
2.   Connection.
3.   Management.

Supervision is required during the various stages of establishing and disconnecting a call through the switched network. Initially the customer's request for service must be detected and dial tone applied to his line (class 5 environment). The called party answer signal must be recognized to initiate call billing, if required.

The calling or called party disconnect must be identified to terminate the call, release equipment, and stop the call charging process. The busy/idle status of trunks are also monitored in order to determine the most efficient routing of a call through the switched network.

The call connection process is initiated by the customer dialing the address of the called party. Upon receipt of this information, the originating local office can determine the proper routing for the call. If the called party is in the same office, then the call is connected across the office to his line circuit.

If the call is destined for another office, then an appropriate outgoing trunk is selected and sufficient address information is transmitted to enable the next office to make the correct connections for the destination of the call.

Other information required to enable a switching office to process a call includes signals to indicate that an office is ready to receive address information and requests for calling party identification for call billing

The management functions, although not necessarily essential for actual call establishment, contribute to the overall efficient maintenance, control, and administration of the voice network. Management functions may comprise one or more signals.

The sophistication of the signaling system determines the amount of network management information that can be made available. Typical applications include:

- Signaling Evolution Network congestion information.
- Alarm and maintenance information.
- Identification of calling party numbers for billing purposes.

Types of Signaling

There is an ever increasing demand for more sophisticated signaling systems to permit the full potential of new generations switching and transmission systems to be realized. The general signaling evolution has been as follows::

1.   DC signaling opening and closing the transmission loop introduced during early mechanical and electromechanical switching products.
2.   AC signaling SF (single frequency) or MF (mullet frequency) tones introduced for common control switching offices.

3.   CCS Common Channel Signaling systems developed for analog and digital stored program switching offices.

Current switching platforms available today utilize primarily the latter two methods defined above; therefore, this document will concentrate on these areas with more time spent on CCS signaling.

DC Signaling

Current systems rarely use DC signaling. Modern systems use more sophisticated signaling formats, see CCS.

AC Signaling

AC signaling systems are primarily used on the inter-toll and toll connect trunks using carrier facilities and generally falls into three major categories:

- SF Single Frequency Signaling uses single tone to convey both address and control information.
- MF Multi Frequency used for address information only.
- DTMF Dual Tone Multi Frequency used for address information associated with customer signaling .

The above systems will not be defined in this document; however, specific information on AC signaling systems can be obtained through the references given in the reference area of this section.

Common Channel Signaling (CCS)

Stored program switches provided faster call processing and more intelligence capabilities in the switched network. However, the full potentials of these capabilities cannot be realized with conventional signaling methods, primarily in the areas of call set-up times and information exchange.

Conventional signaling uses the voice path to transmit the supervisory and control information associated with a circuit connection, whereas the CCS method transfers similar information for a large number of circuits over a data link between the processors of the switches.

CCS provides numerous advantages over current signaling techniques including:

- High speed signaling which reduces post-dialing delay and trunk holding times, resulting in more efficient use of facilities.
- Bi-directional information transfer during voice transmission which can provide calling customer ID before or after the start of conversation.
- Signaling path separate from the voice path which will alleviate fraudulent calling using tone simulation, and interference between voice and supervisory signals.
- Additional information forwarded during the call set-up stage which

may indicate that it is a data call and therefore all bit manipulating devices must be removed or special routing is required.

■   Capability to launch query and response messages to databases which will be required for the introduction of new services such as ACCS (Automated Calling Card Service).

■   Message format flexibility to include signaling information for future new services.

CCS Network Architecture

The architecture for a CCS network is normally based on an administration's unique requirements and the geographical location of the switching offices. Irrespective of the type of architecture selected, the network will consist of a number of switching and processing nodes interconnected by signaling links.

The basic elements include:

Signaling Point (SP): An SP node is normally associated with a switching office. Its prime function is to exchange signaling information between the switch and the CCS network. It administers data flow over the signaling links. Incoming messages are formatted and transferred to the relevant processor in the switching office. Outgoing messages are transmitted over the signaling links.

Signal Transfer Point (STP): An STP node basically performs a message routing function. Incoming messages are examined and routed towards their ultimate signaling point destination. It administers data flow over the signaling links.

An STP may be configured on a "Stand-alone" basis or a switching office may be provided with an STP and SP function which are co-located but physically separate from the switch processor.

In this case, it must have the capability to determine if an incoming message is destined for itself or if it should be transferred forward onto the CCS network. CCS network architecture typically defines an STP as either Regional or Area STPs and all STPs are arranged in pairs for redundancy.

Signaling Link: A signaling link consists of signaling terminal equipment and a signaling data link. It is used for the exchange of information between STs and STPs. These include:

1.   "A-Link" switching offices to their associated Regional of Area STP pairs.
2.   "B-Link" Interconnection of STP's in different regions.
3.   "C-Link" Regional STP to its mate STP.
4.   "D-Link" Area STP pair to its associated Regional STP pair.

5.   "E-Link" switching office directly to a Regional STP in another region.
6.   "F-Link" - Between switching offices in the same or in a different region.

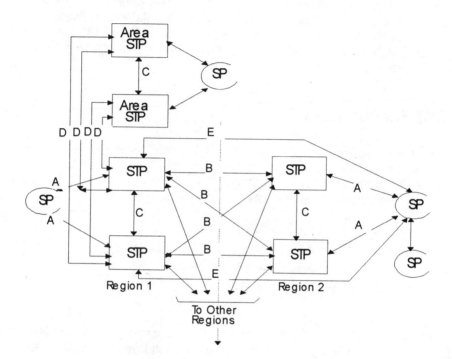

Figure 22: SS7 Signaling Network

CCS7/SS7 Overview

In North America, CCS7/SS7 is the present day Common Channel Signaling standard to which digital networks are evolving. CCS7 is based on the CCITT#7 specification.

The CCS7 system uses 56/64 Kbit/s signaling links and is based on a layered protocol concept. Currently, seven levels are defined: Levels 1, 2 and 3 are called the Message Transfer Part (MTP) and are concerned with the reliable transport of the signaling information.

Levels 4, 5 and 6 are called the Application Service Part and provide a set of common features to enable the effective use of the MTP by its user's applications. Level 7 is the Application Part which serves the different applications (users) of the CCS7 system. The signaling information is conveyed in blocks of variable length consisting of an integral number of bytes up to a maximum of 256 bytes.

A special protocol called Mobile Application Part (MAP) specifies the signaling functions used for handling information specifically related to roaming Mobile Stations. Each node in the network (MSC, VLR, HLR, AUC, EIR) uses Mobile Application Part protocols to transfer signaling information between itself and the other nodes.

CCS7 Functional Layers

Each of the Application Entities, including the MSC, contains software that corresponds to CCS7 functional architecture, which uses several layers to describe the interconnection and exchange of information between CCS7 users. The CCS7 layers, which use the physical layer, are as follows:

- Message Transport Part (MTP) Layer.
- Signaling Connection Control Part (SCCP) Layer.
- Transaction Capabilities Application Part (TCAP) Layer.
- Mobile Application Part (MAP) Layer.

A layer in one Application Entity logically communicates with its peer layer in another Application Entity. Physically, however, each layer communicates only with adjacent layers within its own Application Entity.
The following is a brief description of the layers.

Message Transfer Part (MTP)

The Message Transfer Part layer of CCS7 serves as a connection less transport system between locations of communicating users. The term "user"s, in this case, refer to the Application Entities, which utilize the basic transport capability provided by the Message Transfer Part layer.

Signaling Connection Control Part (SCCP)

The Signaling Connection Control Part (SCCP) layer of CCS7 provides routing of messages between users within a telecommunication network. SCCP is used by TCAP (the next higher level) as a message transport mechanism. The SCCP layer recognizes each Application Entity as a separate subsystem.

Transaction Capabilities Application Part (TCAP)

The TCAP is the interface to Mobile Application Part procedures. The Mobile Application Procedures interface uses this layer, as well as the lower two layers. The TCAP consists of functions that control non-circuit-related information transfer between nodes.

The TCAP ensures that units of information to be exchanged are formatted and exchanged properly. It provides encoding and decoding rules for the information exchange. It also associates each TCAP message and the information it contains with a particular type of application process transaction.

This transaction association enables the TCAP to link a query with a response and identify the context.

Mobile Application Part (MAP)

The Mobile Application Part layer uses the MTP, SCCP, and TCAP layers to transfer information among Application Entities. The Mobile Application Part protocols are responsible for the following:

- Defining the Application Entities.
- Defining the interfaces between the Application Entities.
- Defining the network configuration of the Application Entities.
- Defining the signaling functions required for using CCS7 to provide the services needed by voice and non-voice applications in the network.

Network Connectivity

PSTN Interconnectivity

PSTN interconnect options will see the initial deployment of standard Channel Associated Signaling (CAS) with future deployment utilizing CCS as technical and regulatory issues are further solved.

Intra-Switch Connectivity

As the operator's PCS network evolves, multiple switches will be installed to cover geographic and capacity driven requirements. The long term plan will see

all of the operator's switches directly interconnected utilizing a combination of leased and private facilities.
Within any major metropolitan area (i.e., Toronto), multiple switches will ultimately be used to cover the entire area. Because these switches will have coverage area adjacent to each other, direct trunks must be in place to support roaming and inter-switch handoff.

Inter-switch Interconnectivity will be facilitated utilizing CCS signaling over the operator's facilities.

Advanced Intelligent Network (AIN)

Intelligent networks have already become well established in wireline networks for the provision of advanced features and services. However, the ability of an IN architecture to provide customized services is particularly valuable to the PCS user, who can have improved control over the handling of incoming calls.

Key points to investigate into the design and deployment of AIN functionality in the operator's network include:

- Recognition and comprehension of a North American industry standard for design and deployment of AIN network functionality.
- Conformance and application of network elements to a North American AIN architecture and interface protocol specification.
- AIN network architecture and design i.e., redundancy of AIN network elements
- The role of the SS7 signaling network in the support of AIN features and functionality.

It is expected that AIN products will play a strategic role in a PCS service provider's offerings. The operators may choose to deploy their own AIN components, or alternatively utilize existing wireless or wireline AIN elements when and if regulatory environments permit.

The use of existing AIN elements along with strategic deployment of key wireless AIN nodes will provide a greater level of ubiquitous coverage between the wireline and wireless networks.

Asynchronous Transport Mode (ATM)

ATM is a natural evolution for many types of telecommunications, wireless or PCs being no exception. ATM technology is a specific packet oriented mechanism for the transfer of digital information which is highly compatible with the format of proposed digital access technologies.

Because of this, further investigation will be required to understand the role ATM may play in the operator's PCS switching network but it is apparent that a number of applications using ATM will be applicable to fixed transmissions systems.

11

Network Infrastructure

System Overview

Equipment Supplier Qualification
Standards Participation

An operator's equipment supplier must be active in all relevant standards bodies within North America. The intent is therefore threefold:

1. To facilitate interconnection between different users and platforms
2. To facilitate the portability of equipment within different applications and regions, such that market size is increased, resulting in reduced cost due to economies of scale.
3. To ensure that equipment bought from one vendor can interface to that from another. This may benefit the operators by enabling competitive procurement.

The intent is to ensure that the operator's network will be provided with independent signaling functions and Intelligent Network (IN) architectures and concepts for the technology platform chosen. The outcome of this requirement will be a more "open," flexible and feature rich environment which will increase the usage and popularity of the operator's PCS network.

Standards bodies include:

- TIA: Telecommunications Industry Association.
- IEEE: Institute of Electrical & Electronics Engineers among others.

Approach

It is assumed that the chosen vendors will be industry leaders and will have proven experience in many of the following areas:

- MSC design and planning.
- AMPS cellular.
- Digital cellular (Digital AMPS, IS-54, TDMA, CDMA, etc.).
- ISDN/SS7.
- AIN Development.
- Radio Infrastructure Design, Development and Manufacturing.
- Residential Services.
- Voice Messaging.
- Network Integration.

Vendors bringing experience such as this should give the operators a proven technology and valued differentiation required for success.

Vendors GSM/TDMA/CDMA Solution

Northern Telecom GSM / CDMA
Switching Network Infrastructure HLR STP/SCP
END User Services

AT&T TDMA / CDMA
Switching Network Infrastructure HLR STP/SCP
END User Services

Ericsson GSM
Switching Network Infrastructure HLR STP/SCP
END User Services
and others.

Switching Platforms Industry Examples

Northern Telecom DMS-MSC

The DMS family of digital switches manufactured by Northern Telecom has variants designed to meet the requirements of all levels in the network hierarchy. The DMS SuperNode Switching Family includes local, and tandem trunk and international PSTN exchanges.

The DMS SuperNode hardware structure is based on a distributed processing architecture organized into six functional elements:

- DMS-Core and DMS-Bus.
- Input / Output controller.
- Switching Network, made up of microprocessor controlled, digital switching Network.
- Modules that interconnect the Peripheral Modules, using TDM.
- Microprocessor controlled Peripheral Modules.
- SuperNode systems that employ a mixture of DS30 and DS512 optical fiber links. Similarly, the message links are either DS-30 or DS512 but with all channels used for message data.

AT&T #5ESS

The AT&T 5ESS 2000 switch platform provides the PCS switching function that manages the connectivity between the PCS Base Stations and the various networks. In addition, this PCS platform supports both wireless and wired applications.

The PCS switch is engineered to support the expected traffic loads (at the specified blocking) of the various call types (voice, data, FAX) up to the engineered capacity of the platform. Depending on these traffic loads some number of traffic handler channels and network trunks will be equipped.

The 5ESS supports up to 192 switching modules (SM). Each 5ESS-2000 Switching Module supports up to 3600 trunks. In addition, the 5ESS provides a number of remote options that allow the operator to optimize the trunking arrangements as required.

Ericsson AXE

The AXE system from Ericsson is widely deployed throughout the world. AXE supports a complete range of telecommunication network applications. It is fully digital and designed to minimize overall network and handling costs. Stored program control provides for an open-ended supply of new features and services.

The AXE architecture is a five level hierarchy, each level made up of specific modules. These are defined as follows since the entire AXE system is a set of specified functions:

- System level 1
- System level 2
- Subsystem level

- Function Block level
- Function unit level

The above levels are implemented in modules, or function blocks. These function blocks are grouped in subsystems. Each function block and subsystem is considered a 'black-box' at its specific level in the system hierarchy.

A typical function block consists of a hardware unit, a regional software unit, and a central software unit. Communication between function blocks is carried out by means of software signals. A typical AXE telephone exchange is built up of 400 to 500 function blocks.

System Capacity and Expansion Capability

Summary of Capacity Plan

Capacity requirements of the PCS network will ultimately be driven by market penetration (number of subscribers) along with the offered traffic per subscriber. Network capacity is determined through traffic calculations made on the basis of a minimum grade of service (GOS) which the network is designed to support.

Ultimate System Capacity

There are effectively two key limits on system capacity: (1) the amount of traffic that the switches can carry and (2) the amount of control that the processor can exercise without the occurrence of unacceptable losses. Limit 2, the amount of control that the processor can exercise without excessive losses, can be broken down as follows:

1. *Ultimate capacity due to traffic load:* Traffic capacity consists of two parameters, the number of calls per hour λ, and their duration $1/\mu$. The average call is about 120 seconds (i.e., $1/\mu = 120$). The physical limits of switching capacity are reflected in the number of trunk interfaces and the traffic load a.

2. *Ultimate capacity due to control:* Processor control operates on a delayed basis when requests are queued or scanned at regular intervals. There are two levels of control. At level 1, processor control is involved in scanning and interfacing with customers. At level 2, central processors are involved when all the data for a call request are received.

Ultimate system capacity limitations are reflected in limits on control, such as the number of calls that the system can handle, including hand-offs, scanning and locating, paging, and assigning a voice channel.

Therefore, the processing capacity for cellular mobile systems is much greater than that for non-cellular telephone systems. In non-cellular telephone switching, the duration of the call is irrelevant, but in a cellular system, it is a function of frequency management and the number of handoffs.

Capacity Parameters

The operators will have to ensure that the capacity of the NSS and BSS are sized to meet projected demand. Subsystem equipment quantities and capacities will be designed to meet the requirements of the projected subscriber base. Technology enhancements and improvements (i.e., half rate coding, compression improvements) may be utilized throughout the deployment and operations period to ensure adequate network capacities.

The specific parameters that can determine the maximum limits and capacities include but are not limited to:

- Active Subscriber Ratio.
- Successful Traffic per Subscriber in Busy Hour (Erl).
- Successful Call Holding Time (seconds).
- Unsuccessful Call Holding time (seconds).
- Busy Hour Call attempts (successful).
- Busy Hour call attempts (unsuccessful).
- Mobile Originating traffic.
- Mobile terminating traffic.
- % of local traffic.
- % of toll traffic.
- % of international toll traffic.
- % of calls using supplementary services.
- Number of SMS (short message service) per sub in busy hour.
- IMSI (International Mobile Subscriber Identity) attaches per subscriber in BH.
- IMSI Detaches per subscriber in BH.
- Intra-BSC handovers per call in BH.
- Inter-BSC handovers per call in BH.
- Inter-MSC handovers per call in BH.
- Inter-Location Area Location Updates per sub in BH.
- Inter-VLR(MSC) location updates per sub in BH.
- Inter-PLMN location updates (Roaming) per sub in BH.

The above characteristics specifically determine the capacity of the Mobile

Switching Center. MSC capacity is generally defined with the following high-level parameters:

- T1/PRI: Maximum number of T1/PRI's for interconnectivity into the PSTN (NT GSM theoretical maximum = 3488 T1s).
- A-Interfaces: Maximum number of interface ports between the MSC and the BS components (NT GSM theoretical = 150).
- Subscribers: Maximum number of subscribers that can reside actively on the MSC (NT GSM theoretical = 280,000, practical = 175K).
- Location Areas: Maximum number of location areas.
- Maximum BTS configuration: Maximum number of base stations that can be supported by the MSC.
- Maximum Routes: Maximum number of routes allowable.
- BHCA (Busy Hour Call Attempts) - Minimum number of Busy Hour Call Attempts supported by a fully configured MSC.

Network Capacity Forecast

Network capacity will be initially engineered to marketing projections and forecasts of required coverage area, and subscriber counts. The following table indicates the type of table that can be used for the projected subscriber forecast along with the network capacity in each of the first three years of operation.

Year	1997		1998		1999	
Region						
#BTS - sectored						
#BTS - omni						
#BSC*						
#Channels						
Capacity (Erl)						
Capacity (Subs)						
Total Capacity						

Figure 23: Network Capacity Table

The above table can provide a summary of capacities involved and can give a head start to both RF switching and transmission engineers.

Spectrum Availability

2 GHz Relocation

On June 9, 1994, the FCC modified its 2 GHz PCS spectrum allocations (DC-2613, General Docket 90-314) changing the way the 2 GHz Fixed Microwave Service incumbents will be affected. The highlights of that decision are as follows:

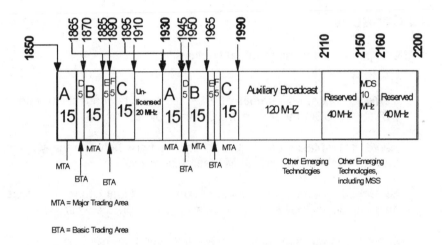

Figure 24: Spectrum Allocation

1.   All licensed and unlicensed PCS spectra are now consolidated within a single band from 1850 to 1990 MHz. This reduces the number of affected 2 GHz hops by about 3000 hops in the main population centers in Canada and 4700 hops in the United States.

2.   Microwave links operating between 2110 and 2200 MHz will eventually have to relocate as well (by July 1997 in Canada).

3.   The FCC is now directing its attention to the competitive bidding rules for broadband PCS (2 GHz licensed PCS) in the 1850 to 1910 and 1930 to 1990 MHz bands. Spectrum auctions that started in the United States early in 1995 have now been completed. Although the unlicensed PCS spectrum is reduced by half, the UTAM (Unlicensed PCS Committee for 2 GHz Microwave Transition and Management) relocation timetable has not been affected.

4.   The construction time requirements for both 30 MHz and 10 MHz PCS license holders (20 MHz blocks no longer exist) are relaxed. Licensed PCS (1850 to 1910/1930 to 1990 MHz) providers will have longer to build up their systems.

5.   Maximum power level permitted for Broadband PCS base stations has been increased to allow larger PCS cells, which could increase interference with incumbent 2 GHz microwave users.

Network Elements Capacity Specifications

MSC Capacity

The MSC capacity is described with the following parameters:

■   *T1/PRI:* Maximum number of T1/PRI's for interconnectivity into the PSTN (NT GSM theoretical maximum = 3488 T1s).

■   *A-Interfaces:* Maximum number of interface ports between the MSC and the BS components (NT GSM theoretical = 150).

■   *Subscribers:* Maximum number of subscribers that can reside actively on the MSC (NT GSM theoretical = 280,000, practical=175K).

■   *Location Areas:* Maximum number of location areas.

■   *Maximum BTS configuration:* Maximum number of base stations that can be supported by the MSC.

■   *Maximum Routes:* Traffic routing.

■   *BHCA (Busy Hour Call Attempts):* Total number of Busy Hour Call Attempts generated from Mobile Originating calls and incoming calls from the PSTN.

Figure 25 summarizes key MSC capacity limits for a NORTEL DMS switch as well as an ATT 5ESS switch. Please be aware that the capacity limits from manufacturers are continuously under review. Manufacturers reserve the right to change their specifications at any time.

The MSC capacity limits are given here only as a guide and should not be used for design work. If detailed capacity limits are required, then the reader should obtain the up to date information from the individual switch manufacturers.

Description	NT -DMS (VS-70)	AT&T #5ESS
Max # Cells	117/BSC	N/A
Max # Sites	39/BSC	222
Max # Trunks	3488 T1s	17000
Max # BHCA	166700	200000
Max # Routes	1000	Not Known
Max # Subscribers	280000	Varies

Figure 25: MSC Capacity Table

MSC Performance

MSC performance will vary dramatically depending on call processing and related overhead requirements.   Important factors directly impacting MSC performance include:

Call Processing (Call Attempts)

Active Subscribers

- Roaming subs

Mobility Management

- Location updates
- Handoffs
- Interim MSC
- Inter BSC

Maintenance & Overhead

- Provisioning
- Billing

■   Network maintenance

Consideration must be given for the MSC platform to have a scaleable architecture which can provide expanded capacity through on-board processor software and hardware upgrades. Further consideration must also address MSC evolution in the ability of the switching platform to off-load processes (i.e., billing, operations, etc.) to external Application Processors (APs) as real-time processing requirements exceed realistic capacity limits.

HLR Capacity

The HLR function can reside either as an integrated component of the MSC (i.e., MSC/HLR INODE Configuration) or as a stand-alone processor accessed through high speed links.

HLR capacity is typically defined by the number of subscribers that can be effectively maintained in the HLR database, along with the number of inquiries per second that can be processed.

An assumed average of 0.5 HLR queries per call (mainly relating to mobile terminating calls) in busy hour (assume BHCA to be 125,000) will effectively translate into approximately 18 HLR queries per second per switch.

The size of the HLR is generally limited by the available memory along with the real-time processing ability. Typical data requirements per subscriber are in the area of 120 words/sub (NT - GSM specs) assuming that new features will double the per sub data requirements, 200 to 250 words per subscriber should be assumed. (i.e., 250K subs * 250w/sub= 62.5M words of memory).

Traffic Forecast

Network traffic projections must be determined on a per subscriber basis in the following areas:

● Mobile Originating traffic	xx.xx mErl.
● Incoming Traffic from PSTN	xx.xx mErl.
● Mobile Terminating Traffic	xx.xx mErl.
● Outgoing traffic to PSTN	xx.xx mErl.
● Traffic terminating to voice mail Service.	xx.xx mEr. or Short Message
● Mobile to Mobile Traffic	xx.xx mErl.
● Miscellaneous Traffic	xx.xx mErl.
● Lost Traffic	xx.xx mErl.
● Internal Traffic	xx.xx mErl.

Percentage of BHCA traffic mobile generated   xx%
Percentage of BHCA traffic mobile terminated xx%
Average effective call duration   x seconds
BHCA per mobile subscriber   x.x

The above traffic patterns are graphically illustrated in the following diagram (Figure 26).

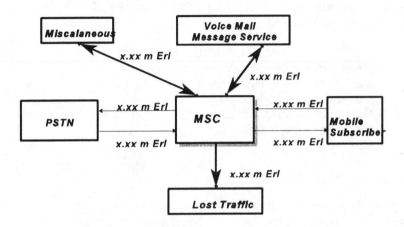

Figure 26: Illustration of Traffic Patterns

BSS Capacity Specifications

BSS capacity can be defined by examining the specific capacity limits of the major network elements which incorporate the BSS subset.

Transcoder Equipment (TCE)

The Transcoder Unit (TCU) is generally used to reduce the number of links needed to convey radio speech and data channels between BTSs, BSCs and MSC.

The following capacity limits may be used to examine TCE capacity. Note that use of a separate TCE network element is vendor dependent and will have to be evaluated on a platform basis. Capacity of a TCU is typically determined by the following:

- Maximum number of traffic channels per interface
- Base Station Controller Equipment (BSC)

BSC
In a PCS network, the Base Station Controller (BSC) provides the link between radio sites. This includes the base transceiver stations (BTSs) and the network subsystem (NSS) or MSC.

The following capacity limits may be used to determine BSC capacity.

Note that use of a separate BSC network element is vendor dependent and will have to be evaluated on a platform basis. Capacity of a BCU is typically determined by the following:

- Maximum number of full rate channels
  - Maximum number of half rate channels
  - Max number of A interfaces
  - Max number of M-interfaces
  - Maximum number of CCS7 signaling channels
  - Maximum A-bis interfaces
  - Maximum number of RT/BCE

- Maximum traffic (Erl)

Note that it is generally assumed that technological advances in hardware and software will account for expanded capacity through implementation of half rate vs. full rate compression algorithms and technologies.

Base Station Transceiver Equipment (BTS)

- Maximum number of RT (Radio Transmitter) including maximum number of A or Abis interfaces/BTS

- Maximum number of receivers at one receiving antenna including maximum number of RT/Abis interfaces.

12

Network Infrastructure Support

Radio Resource Management

Channel Allocation

Radio channel allocation is performed in the radio subsystem (BSS). When a traffic or data channel is required, the radio channel management must allocate the optimum channel to be used (i.e., lowest interference level, etc.). This function will generally be performed in the BTS equipment.

Voice Activity Detection (VAD) and Discontinuous Transmission (DTX)

VAD enables the speech codes to detect whether a subscriber speaks or not. In the case that there is no speech, the transmitter could be switched off (DTX). DTX may also be used with data transmission if no data are available.

VAD/DTX is a way of reducing average battery consumption of the MS by transmitting only bursts that contain information.

Frequency Hopping

May or may not be applicable.

Operations and Maintenance

Further investigation needs to be completed on the following activities:

Maintenance of Location Registers

Location register (HLR, VLR) maintenance functions provide enhanced protective and restoration means in order to minimize data loss or data inconsistencies in the respective mobile subscriber databases.

Operation and Maintenance Features

Including test systems, software maintenance, performance oriented procedures, etc.

Man/Machine Interface (MMI) Support

The O&M MMI should take advantage of present day graphical user interfaces (GUI) to offer maintenance personnel effective access to O&M functions, with a minimum of learning effort. High level command level interpreters should also be investigated.

Automatic Operator Support

In order to ease command input procedures, the O&M system should provide facilities to define command procedures and support scheduled starts of commands. Command multiplication allowing creation or duplicating of several objects to be initiated by one operator should be supported.

Authorization and Access Control Management

The O&M system should provide means for flexible administration of authorization and access privileges. Access rights should be able to be defined for function (i.e., O&M, Billing) and action levels (i.e., change, list, create) as well as user and user groups.

Configuration Management

Further investigation needs to be completed on the following activities:

Installation Support

O&M functions should include support of the installation or upgrade of new hardware and software. Installation of new, update of old, extension as well as reconfiguration of existing equipment must be addressed.

Build Control

The ability to perform compatibility checking between existing hardware and software versions must be addressed.

The software compatibility should apply not only on the applications software but also on the operating system software version.

Administration of Subscriber Data and Equipment

The ability to administrate changes to subscriber data and subscriber equipment changes must be investigated. Administration and Control of System Data

Administration and updating of all software and data including MSC, BSC, BTS, and all other peripheral loads. Change management and software logging for re-configuration of modified parameters as well as activation schedulers for software and data modifications needs to be investigated.

System Time and Calendar Handling

The administration of system time and date. The O&M system should provide for total system time and calendar handling, including multiple time zones, time synchronization, etc..

Performance Management

Performance Measurements

The ability to provide specific system performance information such as processor load, traffic profiles, call processing events needs to be addressed. Further , the ability to format and schedule reporting of performance measurements will be a requirement.

Fault Management

Further investigation needs to be completed on the following activities:

Fault Detection and Diagnosis

The network needs to support automatic detection, localization, and isolation of system faults and failures. Automatic reconfiguration, failure tracking and repair control facilities should be addressed.

Alarm Handling

System alarms need to be collected, presented in an appropriate way, and evaluated statistically for further information. The capability should exist which allows alarms to be routed to and displayed on designated terminals. Log files and log file analysis should be provided.

Maintenance Support

Maintenance support functions should be available remotely and on-site for hardware and software maintenance.

Canadian Interconnection Arrangements Summary

Public Cordless Telephone Service

The PCTS industry today is governed by the current Bell Canada PCTS Tariff (CRTC 7396, Special Facilities Tariff G-255) which provides the central office equipment and facilities necessary to interconnect to the Public Cordless Telephone Service Provider's licensed Public Cordless Telephone Service with the Bell Canada public switched telephone network.

The tariff consist of three major areas

1.   Access Numbers: A 7 digit telephone number with outpulsing from a Bell Canada used in association with Megalink Service (CRTC 6716, General Tariff Item 5200). The key component of the Megalink service as it relates to this area of the PCTS Tariff is the $.16 phone numbers.

2.   Digital Network Access: Access between the PCTS operators mobility office and the PSTN is again provided by the Megalink Service. Megalink Service is based on ISDN primary rate interface standard. The service consists of 23 B channels and an associated D channel for signaling and control.

3.   Distribution Network: Calls originating from the PSTN and processed in the PCTS Mobility Switch will be completed on an analogue basis to the Integrated Base Station utilizing Centrex III (CRTC 6716, Item 670) functionality.

The combination of the three major areas and the associated tariff for each has resulted in a tremendous expense for the PCTS operating company.

The cost of a Primary Rate Interface priced by the Megalink tariff wipes out any gain from a $.16 phone number. An operator (if existed) would use very little of the ISDN functionality that is associated with the Megalink.

The use of Centrex III to connect the Base Stations to the PSTN is considerably more than just a local PSTN 7 digit number. PCTS operators are obligated to use Centrex III locals even though they are not using any of the Centrex Functionality; in fact there is a charge to counter one of the typical Centrex III features (dial "9" insertion).

The additional cost off $8200 per installation that the PCTS operator is required to pay when a new Zone Controller / base station is put into service in a different Bell Wire Center has increased the return on investment time to potential PCTS operators.

Today, none of the licensed PCTS operators are operating a PCTS network in Canada for mainly two reasons. The first reason is that the Canadian standard for PCTS is CT2+, and due to lack of appeal from other countries, NORTEL (the only manufacturer of CT2+ equipment at the time) decided to withdraw its support of this standard for public systems. The second reason is that due to the recent awards of the PCS licenses in Canada, the PCTS operators decided to concentrate on PCS due to the larger market share, and drop PCTS instead.

Cellular Service Operators

In comparison the Cellular Access Service Type I (CRTC 7396, Special Facilities Tariff G-250) allows cellular companies to interconnect to the PSTN via digital access via a Megaroute Service (CRTC 6716, General Tariff 5020). The cost of the cellular phone number is higher ($.80) but the cost of the digital access is less and there is no Centerx III costs or considerations to account for.

Both the cellular operating companies and the PCTS operating companies are limited by the existing tariffs in the types of services & features that they can utilize from the Stentor member telephone companies and Bell Canada.

Neither the cellular nor PCTS operator has trunk side access, therefore no access to the Stentor / Bell Canada CCS7 / STP network. The two national cellular companies (Bell Mobility and Cantel) are currently negotiating IS-02 which would give them CCS7 interconnection. However the time line for this agreement seems to be some time away.

PCS

The PCS operator's intention is to build a network infrastructure which will compare to the existing cellular companies and Interexchange Carriers. The

PCS network will be composed of Mobile Switching Centers (MSC) located in strategic areas around the country.

The location of these MSCs will depend on population, geographical considerations and the availability of local telco inter-exchange facilities and services.

The PCS infrastructure will not be utilizing the remote access such as a base station/zone controller but will follow closer to the cellular network infrastructure where cell sites will be connected via microwave or fiber facilities to the Mobile Switching Center.

Each MSC will have a interconnect to the local PSTN where calls can be originated and terminated.

The PCS industry would also like to utilize some of the Telco's existing features and facilities that have not been available to the wireless operators to date. Both the cellular and PCS operators would like to interconnect to the Bell / Stentor STP / CCS7 network.

Some cellular operators have built their own CCS7 network allowing their own mobile switches to "talk" but so far have been denied access to the Bell / Stentor STPs.

CCS7 signaling between the PSTN and the mobile switch would greatly increase call set-up and would also reduce the number of "Busy Trunks" on a network by being able to determine if far end facilities are available.

Currently only the Interexchange Carrier's, because of their use of Trunk Side Access, have the option to connect to the Bell Canada/Stentor network.

Canadian CRTC Decision 94-19

Although not directly related to the PCS industry the Canadian CRTC rulings in Decision 94-19 (September 16, 1994) two issues will have a direct impact on the PCS industry as it develops; co-location and the unbundling of services.   Both of these issues will have some effect how the PCS operator builds their network.

"Co-location and unbundling will increase competition, choice and efficient supply, and stimulate the development of competition in local, long distance and enhanced services. unbundling will allow competitors to mix their own components with those of the telephone company in the most efficient manner.

If the PCS industry goes forward and gets IXC status, then the contribution and calculation of such contribution will be of major importance to PCS operators.

Co-Location

Currently, all transmission facilities terminating in the telephone companies central office must be provided by the telephone company. Co-location will allow customers, cellular, PCS or IXCs, the option of physically or virtually terminating their own transmission facilities in the telephone companies central office. Virtual co-location will allow a competitor to terminate facilities at a point outside the central office but provide the same rate and service as a physical co-location.

Co-location with the telephone company in the central office will provide competitors with the option of delivering their traffic to the local central office over leased or owned facilities.

Unbundling of Services

Unbundling of services refers to arrangements whereby competitors are provided with access to the components of the local network (not just the enhanced services) whether those functions are used by the telephone companies or not.

The decision to unbundle services was generally agreed to by all parties involved at the hearings; however the process by which to unbundle was not.

Arguments were heard that services should be unbundled as required by customer request; others stipulated that a time table from the commission must be put in place.

The CRTC ruled in decision 94-19 that all parties must submit to the commission by mid March 1995 a process for the unbudling procedure based on the Ameritech proposal.

Examples of potential unbundled components:

- loops, switches and,interoffice transport,
- SS7 call set-up function,
- signal transport elements of SS7,
- numbering resources (NXXs),
- reciprocal joint traffic arrangements,
- joint installation, maintenance and testing functions.

How co-location and utilization of the unbundled services will effect the PCS operator will depend greatly on the submissions of the telephone companies and the ensuing policy that the CRTC issues with respect to those submissions.

Conclusions

Many of these decisions, policies, questions and answers will have an effect on the PCS industry. Such will be the case where a PCS operator should not be limited to the services that they can use to connect their facilities.

The PCS industry will propose that portions of the existing *PCTS tariff*, the *Cellular Access Service tariff* and the *Access Services for Interexchange Carriers tariff* be used in developing the PCS regulatory structure, i.e. the applicable terms, conditions, rates and charges that the PCS industry must follow.

As previously stated the speculation is that the PCS industry will follow the existing Cellular Interconnect IS-01, and instigate the same kind of agreement that the cellular operators are requesting for CCS7 signaling in IS-02.

The Canadian Radio and Television Commission must recognize that for PCS to evolve the principles of an open network architecture and expanded interconnection must be realized by the wire and wireless providers.

As a further development in August 1996, the Canadian government decided to further liberilise the telecommunications market place by allowing (in line with the FCC in the United States) wireline operators to offer cable TV related programming and at the same time allowing cable TV operators to offer telephony services.

Also, in Ocober 1996 it is expected that the Canadian government will also allow smaller operators to instigate a local loop by-pass scenario by awarding fixed wireless local loop by-pass licenses.

Chapter

13

Network Planning

Role of Network Planning in Telecommunications

As a basic requirement, the telephone system must provide for a required quality of communication. This standard can be assessed in terms of the probability of obtaining a connection, the call set-up speed and the quality of speech transmission.

The network upon which the telephone system is dependent comprises switching nodes and transmission and transmission paths, i.e., telephone exchanges, main and local networks circuits and subscriber lines.

Network planning is the continuous, iterative process of monitoring the network, understanding the environment in which the network operates, creating plans which satisfy the demand for existing and new services, implementing those plans and auditing the results.

In order to achieve this function, network planning examines the current network characteristics, forecasts the future network needs, assesses the availability of existing plans, evaluates the technical opportunities for future developments and selects the most appropriate courses of action for long medium and short term.

Network planning must be a continuous process because, for example, achievements may not match the plan; assumptions and constraints will change and technological opportunities will alter and plans will have to be adjusted accordingly.

As forecasts will rarely be absolutely accurate, it is desirable to formulate plans which contain some inherent flexibility. Although this philosophy may give a less than optimum satisfaction of demand, it requires minimum adjustment to the plans to obtain a satisfactory result should the real situation differ from the forecast.

Although a well planned network can, to some extent, absorb divergence between forecasts (or assumptions) and real occurrences, the degree of this network resilience to change will vary according to many aspects, e.g., network structure, size of network and the pattern and extent of change.

Therefore, in order to maintain an optimum network it has to be continuously monitored and, depending on the degree of change, plans will have to be reviewed and updated regularly. If the best possible utilization of existing plans and future expenditure is to be assured, then it must be accepted that network planning is a continuous iterative process and not a "once and for all" action.

Definition of Network Planning

Network planning consists of the use of scientific methods for optimizing the investments and for dimensioning the equipment in a unified way for the whole country, in order to meet realistic objectives previously defined by the highest level authorities.

These objectives, which will be analyzed in the following sections, aim at both quantitative and qualitative improvements of the present network. They define for example the evolution of:

- the number of subscribers in each area,
- the range of services,
- the quality of service.

Network planning must determine the rules for the use of equipment and for the organization of the network, taking into account technical and economic constraints and ITU and CCIR Recommendations.

From the distribution of the forecast demand, it should develop a schedule of planned actions at each point of the network, in order to satisfy all the objectives with the minimum cost.

Thus, the prime definition of network planning is to provide the right equipment, at the right place, at the right time, and at the right cost in order to satisfy expected demand and give an acceptable grade of service.

Results of network planning must include early forecasting of:

- the necessary financial resources,
- the necessary equipment (procurement policy),
- the necessary manpower (staff policy).

Two kinds of network planning may be distinguished:

- *strategic planning*, which gives guidelines for the basic framework to be followed in the network (structure of the network, etc.),

- *implementation planing*, which gives the particular way to effect investments (definition of projects, etc.).

Each of these provides two kinds of plans:

1. *development plans*, which deal with the quantities of plans necessary to cope with the objectives (for example, new subscribers, or improving quality of service). Each geographical area within the network should have its own development plan.

2. *technical plans*, which deal with the methods used to choose and install equipment in order to guarantee satisfactory operation with regards to the required quality of service. These technical plans are common to the whole network and they must ensure future flexibility of the network and compatibility within the network.

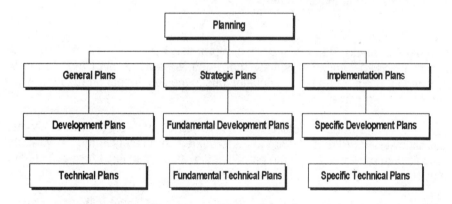

Figure 27: Planning Flowchart

Strategic Plans

A strategic plan charts the direction in which the network is to move over the next 5 to 10 years. It defines the overall framework within which the planning of the various networks, sub-networks (e.g., a rural network) and centers must conform.

Although this plan may comprise various subplans for different networks, they must be coordinated in order to produce a coherent strategy for the future. A strategic plan takes into account telephone traffic growth and distribution, future services and facilities, implications of new technology, financial and service objectives, need for network flexibility, international or national statutory requirements or standards, etc.

In order to give a realistic and homogeneous strategy definition over the whole country, a strategic plan must provide the following general decisions:

■   evolution and completion of the automation of the network (direct dialing for trunk and local networks);

■   network digitalization policy (date of introduction of digital systems for each technical segment of the network);

■   evolution of the fundamental technical plans, particularly evolution of the parameters of grade of service;

■   evolution of the structure of the network (topology, size of centers, hierarchy, etc.)

■   list of possible equipment and ranges of utilization (e.g., specifying that PCM systems will be used between 6 km and 160 km for local links under certain conditions).

Because planning is in practice a compromise between what is seen to be required and the ability to satisfy that need, a strategic plan must often be designed for progressive implementation due to the constraints on resources that may exist at any time.

Modernization strategy could be one example of such an approach. When automatic service (direct dialing) is not provided completely in the network, the strategic plan must determine the percentage of automated lines for each studied year.

Quality of service improvement could be another example. When the present network is very poor, a majority of the links may not comply with currently recommended values for the grade of service. In theses cases, a quantifiable target should be specified for particular points in time within the strategic plan.

For instance, at the 5-year date, it could be stated that there should be less than 20% of links with a probability of loss greater that 0.03; at the 8-year date less than 10% with a loss greater than 0.02 and at the 10-year date less than 5% with a loss greater than 0.01.

Long - Term Plans and Master Plans

Although long-term plans may cover a period of up to 10 years, they may be defined as differing in scope from a strategic plan. Long-term plans relate to specific requirements for a main switching center (including its surrounding area) or to other network components such as transmission or radio links.

The length of these plans is dictated by any long lead time projects, e.g., purchase of sites, erection of buildings, equipment installation, or where changes are not easily made (such as for numbering schemes).

A master plan is a long-term plan extended to a whole local area (a town or a district, for instance). This master plan is required for large investments and the results serve as a target for shorter-term plans of the local area concerned. It contains:

- location and surface area of land required for future building sites,
- floor space and other characteristics of the building,
- capacity of all existing local exchanges,
- need for transit traffic,
- connection to the long-distance network,
- outside plans and buried duct requirements.

Medium-Term Plans and Projects

Medium-term plans might typically cover a maximum of 5 years. They cover plans for equipment which have shorter lead times, as well as extensions of existing switching and transmission systems.

A project is a development plan which defines a schedule of work to be carried out in a given field. Investment optimization and equipment dimensioning must be more precise than previously.

The system which would be most effective in each place is carefully chosen, and transmission and switching installations and extensions are carefully synchronized.

Existing installations and local constraints must be taken into account as well as the objectives of the long-term master plans.

Short - Term Plans and Annual Programs

Short-term plans might typically cover a maximum of 3 years. They include an implementation program which specifies the resource requirements at annual intervals for the total period. For each project an estimation of financial resources is produced. This forms the basis for budget preparation.

Administrators can then make one of the following two possible decisions:

- the plan is accepted, and the next step is the effective implementation of the work;

- the plan is not accepted, and after questioning the objectives or the methods, the plan is prepared again with new hypotheses.

Relations Between Plans

A long-term plan aims to find the economically optimum way to meet the policy objectives based on present cost data foreseeable technology developments. This plan represents a target towards which shorter plans should be directed.

A long-term plan is not a definite commitment to be followed blindly, because it must be updated relatively frequently when changes occur in technology, costs, demand, or resources.

The results of long-term plans may be considered as input data for medium- and short-term planning. For instance, locations of buildings are known for this last stage. In the same way, all the general decisions of strategic plans may be considered as input parameters for shorter-term planning. It is obvious, therefore, that strategic planning and long-term planning must be carefully carried out before commencing shorter-term planning.

In spite of the uncertainty of results of long-term plans, it is necessary to use a long study period (10 years at least) to compare alternative solutions for the development of a network. Many experiences in various countries prove that most of the serious errors in network planning result from a lack of long-term and strategic planning.

With short-term planning only, decisions tend to be made depending on existing plans, and all large investments are postponed as often as possible. This may jeopardize the future, incurring greater running costs and difficulties for the development of the network later.

Successive short-term plans are unable to take account of the benefits of introducing new technologies, or of erecting new buildings. They tend to prolong errors in the structure of the existing network, and the postponed difficulties will later be more costly to solve.

For a strategic plan and a master plan, the target year must be chosen such that existing plans no longer have any influence.

To sum up, short-term plans are not only designed to provide immediate relief where it is required, but also to help meet the objectives of long-term plans.

Each short-term plan must realize a part of the whole investment required by the target network as defined by the long-term plan. The planner must balance his work between carrying out successive short-term plans and updating long-term plans.

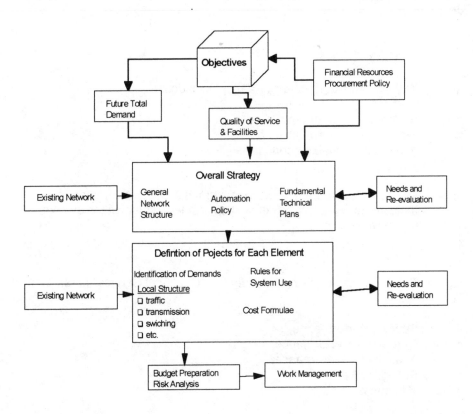

Figure 28: Main stages in network planning

Concept of Quality of Service

The quality of service involves various performance factors. Some may be stated by one or more numerical measures, but an overall measure for the whole network is somewhat utopian.

A quality of service plan requires the Administration to prepare plans for the whole network for each of these performance requirements.

It would be too difficult to try to combine so many different kinds of factors into one comprehensive factor, and would involve many controversial and subjective decisions.

CCITT. 51330

a)   The "service support performance" includes:

- automation with direct dialing,
- waiting list for new subscribers,
- additional available services list.

b)   The term "equipment" is used in a broad sense and it may also indicate, for example, a connection, a telecommunication system, all the network or parts of it.

Figure 28 depicts the subdivisions under the "Quality of Service" parameters. These include:

- Support Performance,
- Operability Performance
- Availability Performance,
- Reliability Performance,
- Transmission Quality.

Under "Availability Performance" we have further parameters that need to be considered as part of the overall planning process. These are:

- Trafficability of Grade of Service,
- Equipment Availability,
- Propagation Performance.

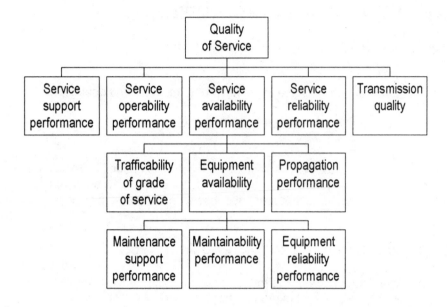

Figure 29: Hierarchy of concepts relevant to the quality of service

Under "Equipment Availability" we have the following parameters:

- Maintenance Support Performance,
- Maintainability Performance,
- Equipment Reliability Performance.

The grade of service provides a numerical measure of network congestion. This congestion is due to insufficient equipment for the offered traffic, and might result either from peak traffic conditions or from network under dimensioning.

This congestion is measured by:

1.   probability of call loss (probability of not obtaining a connection),

2.   pre-dialing delay (time required to return dial tone to the subscriber after a call has been initiated),

3.   post-dialing delay (time interval between the completion of dialing and the receipt of ringing tone.).

The concept of service is fundamental to network dimensioning.

Administration Aims in Network Planning

The Administration's aims in network planning are the following:

- to improve the service in terms of both quantity and quality,

- to make telecommunication services as economically efficient as possible.

These two aims may be contradictory in some situations. For example, improvement of the waiting time for providing service to new subscribers may require huge investments that present subscribers do not wish to pay.

Organization, Optimization, and Architecture

Network organization comprises the minimizing of the quantity and unit cost of equipment only used for a limited number of subscribers and the increasing of the quantity of equipment which will be shared by many subscribers.

Network optimization consists of choosing the number of switching nodes and the transmission links which connect these points, so as to minimize the total investment, taking into account various criteria and constraints.

For example, the number of switching centers results from finding the minimum total costs of subscribers' lines, circuits, and switching centers.

Network architecture is established according to the traffic flows (dispersal of traffic over a large number of directions) outgoing from each switching center.

These flows considered as too small for creating a direct circuit group are put together on common circuit groups towards a transit center.

New PCS operators that have just entered the wireless world (such as the C Band players in the United States) would probably want to be physically the closest to the transit center of their respective long distance partner.

This physical proximity to the transit center would allow them to minimize their transmission costs.

Fundamental Technical Plans

Availability and Security Plans

These plans are ways of maintaining the quality of service offered to the customer. Availability objectives refer to the amount of time an item is ready for use (including factors such as reliability) and security methods refer to the ability of calls to reach their destination in the event of item failure (including standby systems, etc.).

Availability plan objectives should be specified for separate network components as well as for the whole network as seen by the customer.

The security plan must list the equipment items which would have the greatest effect on the network if they were to fail, and the alternative methods chosen to maintain network availability.

Traffic Routing

This plan must determine how the traffic carried in the network is routed from any subscriber to any other. The basic principle is to use a path according to the upward and downward hierarchy.

The hierarchy should be defined first, i.e., for each level, the number of centers, their location and their boundaries of influence are specified.

Area definitions must be achieved both by trying to group together all the centers having the most important affinities, and also by taking account of the interactions with the other fundamental technical plans (switching, dialing, etc.).

The second act is the definition of rules for connecting between the various levels:

- providing a direct or high usage route when traffic is insufficient,

- following the hierarchical path (final routes), which allows the grouping of all the low traffic routes up to the next exchange where the same network planning problem may occur again.

Signaling Plan

The aim of this plan is to define the methods and signals to be sent between exchanges to set up calls, for sending call charging information, and for other administrative purposes. Interfaces must be provided between different types of systems to convert signals.

Signaling systems can be classified into two kinds of signals:

1.   line signals, which have a very important influence on the transmission equipment,
2.   the signals between registers (dialing) which have a very important influence on the switching equipment.

Between the possible solutions for the line signaling there is the following choice:

■   in band, or out band,
■   by pulse code, or by direct current signals.

A signaling plan must choose the most suitable route for the network.
It is also necessary for signals between registers to choose between using pulse code methods of one of two frequencies, and multi-frequency methods.

The present tendency is towards common channel signaling since the introduction of SPC.

Numbering Plan

This plan aims at giving an exclusive number to each subscriber for the automatic setting up of a communication. This plan must certainly be prepared far in advance and with much care, as it is the most difficult and expensive to modify later, because of both the resulting equipment modifications necessary in the switching centers, and changes in the customer's behavior.

Consequently, this plan must be prepared before beginning the long distance network automation process and must last at least 30 and typically 50 years.

A numbering plan must be designed according to the following criteria:

■   ease of use and understanding for all the subscribers,

■   compatibility with existing and future equipment,

■   compatibility with international norms,

■   ease of setting up traffic routing and charging plans,

■   taking into account expanding traffic of subscribers.

Transmission Plan

This plan aims at specifying the transmission quality between subscribers, once the communication is up. The first objective of a transmission plan is to establish an overall reference equivalent which also takes other degradations into account such as frequency and phase distortion, echo crosstalk and other types of noise, and to distribute such degradations in the best way possible in the network.

In particular, the transmission plan must specify which transmission arteries will be 2-wire and which will be 4-wire. The tolerated attenuation standard values must take account of:

- the number of levels in the switch center hierarchy,
- the local area size,
- expansion considerations due to volume increase.

For local distribution and transmission the aim is to use small gauge cables, which are less expensive. To this end, the long distance network must be designed to have the least possible attenuation in order to leave the maximum available for the local network.

Typically OC-48 (2488.32 Mbps) or higher backbone speeds are designed for inter-city transmission paths. Normally this also includes backbone redundant rings.

Lately most of the transmission infrastructure is based on fiber optic cable access to both residential and commercial sites. This will allow the ability to implement intelligent residential and commercial gateways into the homes and small businesses.

By utilizing advanced new generation residential gateways with fiber inputs, customers will benefit by having high speed data, full motion digital video, alarm monitoring, telemetry for their utility meters, and, of course a number of voice channels all coming into their homes.

Of course the implementation of high speed fibre access points into the residential and small commercial markets, will require high speed backbone networks capable of satisfying the high future requirements.

All of the above need to be taken into account when planning a transmission network.

Synchronization Plan

A synchronization plan is needed in a digital network to meet the slip rate objective.

It must therefore specify the frequency accuracy at each clock, together with the synchronization methods used. Typically, a stratum 3 or 4 source is used as a primary clock input.

The clock accuracy effectively defines the slip rate, and the slip rate objective is the main feature of synchronization affecting the quality of service to the customer. (The effect of a given slip rate is different for different services, and different objectives for different services may therefore be appropriate.)

Charging Plan

Local call charging can use various methods:

- fixed charges, independent of the number of calls, their holding time and their distance within the local area,
- charges according to the number of calls only,
- charges according to the number of calls, their holding time and distances.

Long distance communication charges can vary with duration and from one country to another depending on the Administration's plan.

In Europe, a number of countries use "pulses" as part of their charging plan. A "pulse" corresponds to a unit price and it is related to duration.

Determining a tariff plan includes government decisions, but network planners would normally have a role in supplying the cost component structure to which the tariff structure should correspond.

It should be noted that tariff modifications or even some tariff characteristics can heavily influence the network traffic evolution. This will have to be carefully taken into account in the planner's traffic forecasting methods.

Most wireless operators especially the new PCS entrants will have to come up with some very entreprizing charging plans in order to attract new subscribers.

It would be interesting to see some of the developments and new ideas resulting from creative marketing departments towards the end of this century which will result in some interesting charging plans..

Switching Plan

For all types of switching centers from the smallest remote exchange concentrators to the largest transit changes, the essential characteristics must be specified:

- subscriber, traffic and calls capacities,
- traffic routing capability (number of trunk groups and overflow ability),
- 2- or 4-wire switching,
- signaling,
- accommodation and power requirements.

Planning Process

Demand Forecasting

Demand forecasting consists of specifying the evolution of the number of subscribers to be connected and the quantity of traffic to be carried, at each point in the network and for each year. This evolution results from two successive compromises:

The first compromise is between the total investment of all types and the amount of investment in telecommunications, which will be selected by the political authorities according to the priority that telecommunications are given. The economic resources of a country can limit the total amount available to satisfy the telephone demand.

The second compromise must be made between the number of subscribers connected and the quality of service provided: a delicate choice when equipment is in short supply. If the quality of service is too low compared to the desirable norms (in some cases, recommended by ITU), then telecommunications may not meet the basic needs, although this represents a priority decision to be made by the Administration.

However, it may be noted that a poor quality of service often leads to equipment overload, which in turn aggravates the quality of service degradation. In the extreme, most exchanges and circuit groups will be carrying traffic which cannot be effective because of the general and nearly permanent congestion.

In an automatic network with under dimensioned equipment, the phenomenon of call reattempt leads to a very low level of network economy.

Once the overall objectives concerning the year-by year quantity and quality requirements have been determined for the period under study, the forecasting work consists of calculating the evolution of demand at a sufficiently detailed geographical level to provide the data necessary for dimensioning particular exchanges and circuit groups.

With the advent of PCS it is feared that due to the financially demanding environment in wireless communications, quality will be compromized at least during the initial stages of deployment. It remains to be seen whether this would be the case or not.

Traffic Forecasting

Methods of dimensioning and optimization of networks rely upon traffic forecasts, which themselves rely upon measurement. In spite of these measurements, knowledge of present traffic and, particularly, of future traffic is insufficient in many Administrations, SPC exchanges should improve this situation.

For dimensioning of exchanges, the following information is required:

- number of call attempts per hour,
- average traffic per subscriber,
- number of subscribers,
- originating and terminating traffic,
- outgoing and incoming traffic,
- number of groups of circuits with size and carried traffic.

For dimensioning the network, an iterative process is necessary, since optimization of the future network structure depends on future traffic between exchanges, and this traffic depends also on the structure of this future network.

As far as dimensioning at the RF level is concerned, wireless operators will have to optimize their RF technologies for best utilization of the available spectrum. Modern digital RF technologies (CDMA, GSM, TDMA IS-136) provide for a varying degree of dimensioning capability.

The evolution of customer behavior is uncertain, and planners must make assumptions for the future average traffic per customer and for the future distribution pattern of traffic between local areas.

Optimization and Dimensioning

The objective of network optimization is to find the best network plan alternative. The problem of optimization is firstly to choose optimization criteria in order to compare different alternatives in a quantitative and objective way.

The following optimization criteria is used:

- the compatibility of the alternative plan with the Administration's aims,
- the compatibility of the alternative plan with policies and strategies,
- economic advantages,
- financial and resource requirements,
- network flexibility,
- technical capability.

The basic method to compare alternative plans from the economic point of view is to calculate present worth annual charges (PWAC) for each plan. These figures would include all the economic events: investment expenditures, operation expenditures and income or savings.

In the long-term this task essentially consists of the determination of the number of exchanges at the various levels of the hierarchy, their sizes, their locations, their service areas, their technology. The traffic routing structure must also be determined, e.g., how to use the transit centers.

From the future traffic matrix, the direct circuit groups and those towards the transit centers are dimensioned in order to minimize the network total cost. This work is complex and requires the assistance of computers; however, by using tables or simple rules, satisfactory (but not ideal) solutions can be found.

In RF transmission future forecasting and dimensioning can be done by using some advanced competerized tools (such as "Planet", and "Comsearch" among others). These tools can forecast the exact number of required cells taking into account subscriber numbers, interference, peak loading as well as many other parameters.

In shorter-term planning, large investments may be considered as input information, given by long-term plans. Moreover, local and technical constraints due to the existing network become preponderant. Because of the multiplicity of possible solutions an overall optimization is no longer possible. Planning is divided into two separate tasks:

1.   traffic routing optimization and circuit group dimensioning,
2.   circuit routing of circuit groups with path and system choices.

For each of these tasks, the planner will have to use a method corresponding to the available data.

For example, very elaborate alternative routing optimizations may be prescribed if enough traffic measurements have been carried out to make sure that the initial matrix is reliable; but they become useless if, for want of sufficient traffic measurements, the initial matrix has been derived from simple theoretical laws.

All the network optimization difficulties rest on how to take account of the various criteria whose variety and contradictory aspects have been emphasized above.

The advantage of a totally manual process is that it affords a better opportunity to integrate some rather subjective criteria, such as the management and operation facilities or network evolution flexibility in the face of unexpected events.

However, as it is absolutely essential to rationalize the investment choices, the methods used involve such complex calculations that a computer is often necessary.

Dimensioning details as far as equipment capability is concerned should be provide by the manufacturers of the supplied equipment. Manufacturers have developed extensive modeling techniques specifically designed for each of the units they supply.

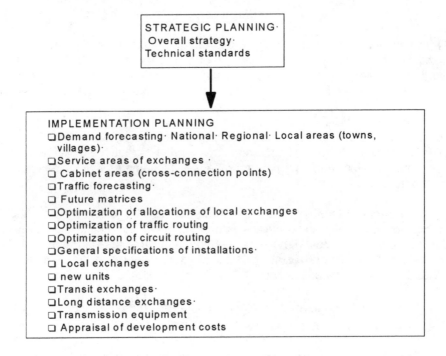

Figure 30: Flowchart of planning process

Standardization of Technologies

It is better for operating companies to standardize the technological choice within the operating area, even though this may seem more expensive from the point of view of investments.

This standardization avoids the need for staff in an elementary area to have a multiplicity of skills, and permits the elimination of some of the problems which arise from the difficult and costly compatibility of some technologies, as for example between digital and analogue systems.

Network Structure Security

Another important objective for the planner is to design the best network structures which offer the best overall security from the given basic technical elements.

According to the resources available, a more expensive solution can be chosen provided the premium is not too great, which gives less troublesome results when an item of switching equipment or a cable breaks down.

For example, a solution in which the switching centers are spread in small units in various places is less risky in the case of a localized breakdown or destruction than a huge switching center. Another example: subscriber line concentrators save copper compared to the use of individual subscriber line connections, but they can be the cause of breakdowns which completely isolate a whole group of subscribers.

Finally, in a multi-exchange network (urban or long-distance) an increase in the number of circuit groups making extensive use of overflowing and multi-routing may make it more possible, at least partially, for traffic to be carried in the case of a breakdown at a particular place, compared with an optimum solution devised only according to investment costs.

Consequently, security is attained on the one hand by spreading the equipment to avoid breakdown due to a localized incident affecting too many subscribers or communications, and on the other hand by being able immediately and automatically to set up another path when the normal one is out of order.

Flexibility of Network Evolution

The planner must not deceive himself that the present hypotheses on which his plans being built will last forever, whether they be traffic data, subscriber forecasts, technologies to be used or cost formulas. These hypotheses can fluctuate narrowly or widely. Some choices which are effectively the best for a present study may not be so after a few years, during the service life of certain equipment.

The planner will have to favor solutions allowing a more convenient adaptation to unexpected situations even if it slightly increases the investment costs.

For example, the consequences of demand forecasting errors can be minimized by modular system which easily enable the necessary extensions to be made as soon as the demand becomes more precisely known.

It also enables the planner to avoid having considerable investments tied up where some will never be used, although they could be used elsewhere.

Another example would be a traffic routing policy which uses more circuits and which improves the network flexibility compared to a proliferation of small direct circuit groups between the exchanges, even though future profitability will not perhaps be as good as expected.

In fact, it should be noted that errors in forecasting traffic are less sensitive on larger than on smaller circuit groups.

Need for a Comprehensive Planning Process

Taking into account the variety of constraints and tasks to be performed, it is not possible to obtain a network development plan with only one attempt at each of the steps presented above.

Consequently, the whole planning process is iterative, and plans are brought into form by proceeding cautiously and making progressive improvements of all the results.

The frequency with which development plans are updated depends partly on the target year, but also on external phenomena such as:

- modifications to overall target year objectives,
- modifications to the budgetary constraints for future years,
- modifications in the apportionment of demand,
- new traffic measurements,
- introduction of new systems, for example digitalization of the network,
- modifications to fundamental technical plans,
- modifications to grade of service objectives.

Consequently, network planning consists of optimizing network development, according to many economic and technical criteria which are sometimes contradictory. The existing network must be used efficiently and this can seem to be contrary to optimization of the final structure.

The planner, while progressively, improving his forecasting system, will have to expect frequent questioning of objectives.

He or she must therefore be prepared for an order to avoid major problems in the future. To this end, the problems must be solved progressively rather than delaying their solution causing many difficulties to arise suddenly and simultaneously.

Consequently, the planner's main concern is to spread harmoniously the investments in space and time:

- in space, by balancing the satisfaction of demand and the grade of service from one point to another of the network, and,
- in time, by balancing the subscribers' immediate and future interests.

Contents of a Routing Plan

General

To plan a network in detail is an immense task. Once alternative plans have been selected, some of the largest computer programs in an Administration's possession may be devoted to optimizing the solution.

The plan itself, even in general terms, would be a very large document, and it is quite possible that an Administration may only be able to lay down general principles, devolving the detailed local routing requirements to its regional planning staff.

The contents of the two main parts guiding rules and specific routings are indicated below.

Guiding Rules

These should include the following:

- the stated planning aim in terms of overall policies towards the maximum number of links in a connection, direct routes, alternative routing, transit routing, hierarchical routing and the implications of any switching, signaling, numbering and transmission conversion plans,

- the community of interest and other guidelines justifying direct routes,

- the maximum number of transit links allowable with particular combinations of switching and transmission,

- the traffic justifying alternative routing, and the number of alternatives before a call takes the final route.

The dimensioning principles for all the route classes consist of:

- subscriber lines, including concentrators and remote switching centers,
- routes between local and primary exchanges,
- direct routes,
- high usage routes,
- overflow routes,
- alternative routes,
- final routes (backbone network),
- minimizing the average number of links on a call.

Specific Routings

For each local area, all routes (paths and sizes) should be specified:

- subscriber lines,
- concentration or remote switching points and equipment used,
- direct routes between local exchanges within the area,
- direct routes to local exchanges outside the area,
- routes between local exchanges and the primary exchange,
- special routes such as operator services, emergency access,
- transit routing,
- alternative routing and the security implications,
- high usage routes,
- overflow routes.

Nationally the following needs to be specified:

- routes between primary exchanges,
- routes to secondary exchanges and between them,
- all other routes in the backbone structure,
- high usage routes,
- overflow routes,
- alternative routes and the security implications,
- possibilities of multilink calls,
- direct routes across international boundaries, avoiding the international exchange,
- access to the international exchange,

■   the number of levels in the hierarchy to give the most economical solution.

Object of a Switching Plan

A switching plan aims to establish the capabilities required from the switch at each node of the network, in a manner best able to provide the services and quality required by the customers and the Administration.

General Considerations

The plan in practice consists of two parts. The first part is the approach during which the services, technical requirements, socio-economic aspects, etc., are defined, and the second part is the study of strategies when the switching methods and their stages of implementation are specified.

It is one of the most complex and expensive aspects of network planning and demands considerable expertise. The ITU manual is entirely devoted to the technical and economic aspects of choosing switching systems.

The switches and controlling equipment in use have many effects on the rest of the network, in terms of its quality, efficiency, topology and versatility. The interactions with other plans are therefore very important and are treated in detail in later sections.

Information to be Presented

The final switching plan should give the following information:

■   general description of the major features, e.g., dates of 50% and of total conversion, exchange type policy, services which will be available,
■   implications for the customers,
■   overall cost - in total and per annum,
■   commercial implications,
■   political/prestige implications,
■   technical benefits,
■   list of exchange types, with their individual conversion policies,
■   any favoring of geographical area, with reasons,
■   reasons for choosing this plan in preference to others,
■   if possible, a detailed list of each exchange's date of conversion, implications on transmission, etc., and so on.

Signaling Planning

Objectives of a Signaling Plan

The prime functions of signaling are to cause the switching systems:

- to alert the called subscriber (or service) and
- accurately to connect the called and calling subscribers.

All the modern complexities of signaling are sophisticated developments of the following basic needs:

- connection of the subscriber to his local exchange,
- direction of the call through subsequent switching centers,
- connection of the subscriber to the called subscriber or service,
- informing the subscriber of progress,
- metering the call, for automatic charging purposes,
- minimizing delays in all functions,
- provision of information for network management (in its broadest sense),
- disconnection of subscribers from their local exchanges on termination of their call,
- freeing the intermediate links and exchanges after call termination.

A signaling plan should achieve the above aims, as required, in the most economically and technically satisfactory manner over the network as a whole.

Contents of a Signaling Plan

A signaling plan should contain the following information:

- list of signals to be exchanged between subscriber and exchange, and between exchanges,
- type(s) of inter register signaling with technical specifications,
- basic type(s) of signaling between subscriber and exchange, with technical specifications,
- geographical and hierarchical coordination of these signaling types to ensure compatibility,
- method of introduction of signaling systems advantage and effects of the plan.

Transmission Planning

Objectives of a Transmission Plan

A transmission plan defines the required transmission quality objectives and how to achieve them for all types of signals.

Perhaps the most difficult aspect of transmission to assess is subscriber satisfaction. Several Administrations have evolved different methods, and the ITU describes several standards. For example, subscribers may be asked "was the call quality good, or poor, etc.?" or simply "did you experience difficulty?" and these results are compared with measurable characteristics. Asking subscribers their opinions is in any case a good public relations exercise

Since some calls use many more links than others, transmission standards must relate both to the worst possible case (and its frequency of occurrence) and to the average call quality.

Required standards are likely to rise as subscribers' expectations of modern technology increase and as wireless operators start claiming that the wireless quality resembles that of the wireline.

A transmission plan should contain the following overall objectives:

- provision of a high quality signal in terms of noise, level and other aspects,
- provision of the best possible service in the prevailing economic climate,
- flexibility for transmission of as many different services as possible.

To be practical and effective it must aim to:

- modernize the network as rapidly and effectively as possible,
- minimize the economic expenditure both in new equipment and temporarily necessary inter-working equipment,
- minimize the technical disruption,
- minimize the need for rapid expansion and contraction of labor forces,
- to be consistent with manufacturing capacity and ability to obtain new equipment.

A transmission plan should contain the following information:

- a complete routing plan showing the distribution of impairments between all nodes, with clear indications of the worst possible cases,
- methods of introduction of new transmission systems,

■   advantages and effects of the plan, with a demonstration of its
     coordination with other plans, and how it can offer good transmission
     quality to any new services which may be introduced,
■   cost of the plan.

Numbering Planning

Functions of Subscribers' Numbers

A subscriber's number has several roles. A major role is to identify the
subscriber uniquely in order to allow a call destined for the subscriber to be
connected to him without risk of confusion.

Secondary roles include:

■   the ability to allow automatic connection between two subscribers,
■   the ability to be easily understood and dialed/keyed by all subscribers,

■   allowing the most efficient usage to be made of switching and control
     equipment,
■   permitting all services, as required by the Administration,
■   allowing international connections to be established,
■   compatibility with a good system of charging,
■   compatibility with plans of adjoining countries as far as is reasonable.

Object of Numbering Plan

A numbering plan is the method whereby the performance of the above
functions is assured by virtue of a correct choice of:

■   number length,
■   national uniformity, or other standard, of number length,
■   an appropriate split between trunk codes, local exchange codes (if
     any) and subscriber numbers,
■   sufficient capacity in the number length to allow for the forecast
     increase in subscribers during the chosen planning period.

The main relationships between the numbering plan and other plans have been
dealt with in previous sections.   For definitions see ITU Recommendation
E.160(35).

Charging Planning

Objects of Charging Plan

The charging plan is the method of charging subscribers for the telecommunications services. A successful charging plan gives:

- subscriber satisfaction,
- adequate revenue consistent with call stimulation,
- adequate return on investment to enable further investment to be made,
- assurances of most efficient use possible of equipment,
- ease of technical implementation,
- ability to relate charges to number of calls made, and/or their duration, and/or their destinations.

Synchronization Planning

Synchronization Concepts

Synchronization of a digital network means meeting the slip rate objective at all digital exchanges. Each exchange has a clock responsible for two actions: on the one hand receiving the streams of bits coming from other digital exchanges, on the other hand controlling the switching part of the exchange and sending the switched bit streams out to other exchanges or ultimately to the users. The word "synchronization" includes both bit timing and frame timing.

Without synchronization, the clocks will certainly differ in frequency. The effect of such differences is that when, for example, a bit stream arriving at an exchange has a frequency higher than the frequency of the exchange clock, not all the bits can be switched directly, but will be temporarily kept in an "elastic buffer".

This is a time slot or frame buffer, accommodating respectively 8 and 193 (24 channel) or 256 (32 channel) bits. when the buffer is exceeded a transmission disturbance occurs, called a slip, which means either that 8 or 193/256 bits of information have been lost or that 8 or 193/256 spurious bits have been inserted into the communications between the users.

An additional aspect of synchronization is frame timing. Frame alignment of multiplexed bit streams is most important in the digital network for time division switching and synchronous digital multiplexing. Frame alignment is realized by:

- frame position detection and phase-adjustment on the multiplexed bit streams,
- absorption of transmission-delay fluctuation by elastic storage.

A good control over slips will be acquired by prescribing solutions in a network synchronization plan. In such a plan an Administration with a digital telephone network will state both the objectives for synchronization performance and the most appropriate methods for achieving this objective.

The planning objective is stated as a maximum allowable slip rate. Such a slip rate may be determined either by studying the sensitivity to slips of the offered services or by use of a general standard, recommended by the ITU as being sufficient for most of the services.

After stating the planning objective, the network synchronization plan describes how the objective should be achieved, in terms of the synchronization method(s) to be used. Each method is particularly convenient in certain networks. The discriminating factors are the size, structure, reliability and cost.

Network Synchronization Methods

Review of Possible Methods

Two different basic principles exist plesiochronous and synchronous.

A **plesiochronous** digital network is one in which the clocks that control the exchanges are independent of each other; however, their frequency accuracy is kept within narrow specified limits.

A **synchronous** digital network is one in which the clocks are controlled so as to run, ideally, at identical rates, or at the same mean rate with limited relative phase displacement.

This terms are fully defined in ITU Recommendation G.702.

Plesiochronous Digital Network

The goal of the synchronous approach is to avoid slips by using some method of frequency or phase control   throughout the digital network.   The most interesting control methods are:

Master-slave, including:

■   hierarchical mater-slave
■   external reference

Mutual:

■   single-ended control
■   double-ended control

The main reason for the interest in frequency control is a long-term potential improvement in economy compared to the plesiochronous operation using very expensive clocks, such as cesium.

Master-Slave Control Method

This is based on the principle of letting one clock act as a master clock. Other clocks are locked (slaved) to the master.

A method using phase locking keeps the phase difference between the master clock and the slave clock constant or even zero. The information about the instantaneous phase difference between the clocks is contained in the elastic buffer at the slave's exchange terminal.

This information is then used in a control circuit (phase-locked loop) to adjust a voltage which controls the slave clock's frequency. This clock is therefore known as a voltage controlled crystal oscillator (VCXO).

The slave clock will thus follow the master, and if the buffer size and control circuits are suitably designed, no slips should occur.

Special cases of master-slave methods are:

■   The hierarchical master-slave method rather than a pure master-slave may be adopted for a meshed network. All exchange clocks are arranged in a hierarchy and every clock is assigned an identification label or rank according to its place in the hierarchy.
     In the case of failure of the master clock as new master having the next highest rank is selected.

■   The external reference method is based on the possibility of handing. A number of sources of precise time and frequency exist, which can be reached via radio, cable, etc. In many cases this distribution of time and frequency information is limited to national boundaries although there are some systems with worldwide coverage.

Availability and Security Planning

Availability Plan

<u>General</u>

When planning a network, the quality of service to be offered to customers should first be defined. It is composed of many different factors, and has been discussed in chapter II. One of those factors is availability and this is discussed here.

The availability plan aims to maintain service quality in case of network failures such as equipment or cable breakdown.

Availability remains a highly theoretical subject and continued research is being undertaken by the ITU/CCIR Joint Study Group on Noise and Availability (CMBD) to render it more practically applicable to telephony

There is an interaction between availability and the grade of service from an overload point of view. The grade of service, or traffic ability, is the switching network ability to meet the requirements of a specified traffic load.

On the other hand, availability is generally defined in terms of particular service levels to be retained in the event of possible system failures. Methods of ensuring such service levels form the security plan.

Overall network availability is a general term relating to the total availability as seen by the subscriber. It includes different concepts such as equipment availability, reliability, maintainability and human factors, and also includes the concepts of network security and of network operation. These factors are contrary to total network economy.

Therefore, one of the most important and difficult aspects of network is to set up a reasonable trade-off point between quality of service and network economy.

Availability Planning

In order to set up and follow an effective availability plan, a total availability objective should be defined and assigned to all network elements.

Different faults give rise to different effects on the network and on the subscriber. They can broadly be divided into service failure or service degradation. Though the fault may be a total equipment failure, efficient security arrangements may mean the final result is no service failure and only slight, if any, service degradation.

There are some failures whose effects are impossible to avoid without great expenditure on security methods. For example, total failure of a primary center will isolate all subscribers in its area from the long distance network, unless standby alternative routes to other primary centers have been provided. The center's long distance transit function may however be transferable relatively easily.

On a smaller scale, efficient design may result in a single unit failure being of little consequence, whereas poor design (large groups of subscribers relying on one piece of equipment is a typical example) can result in service failure relatively frequently

It is, therefore, important for every type of equipment in the network to consider the effect of a failure on service availability, the type of correction most effective, the need for correction, and the cost of the correction method, all based on the concept of a total availability objective.

This objective depends on the network development level, the economic circumstances, the existing telecommunications systems, and so on, in each country. Telecommunication materials and systems should be designed, and network configuration and protection planned, using method based on this objective.

An availability objective should be defined individually for each service: telephony, support systems, data transmission, facsimile, etc. All the different classes of circuits (switched network, point-to point, leased, etc.) should also be considered separately.

The following gives some methods for retaining network availability, mainly from a telephony viewpoint.

Availability and Reliability of Switched Services

For switched services, the concepts of availability and reliability are not so easily applied. In this case, the item is the entire network and the function is really a set of functions, including both call set-up and user information transfer. Conclusions about the ability to perform this functioned to factor in information about the success of set-up attempts, the quality of transmission, and the frequency of unintentional cutoffs.

This section addresses in detail the emerging customer-oriented definition of switched service availability, including how this definition is useful for a customer comparing a switched service with a dedicated service. It also describes how a user of a switched service can evaluate the service's availability without having access to network internal information.

Finally, there is a discussion of how network providers can manage their switched service availability.

Customer-Oriented Definition of Availability

Customers use switched point-to-point communications services in an on-demand fashion, expecting:

- to always be able to establish a new communication path between their terminal and a terminal of their choice,
- to have adequate transmission quality to support their application, and
- to maintain the connections long enough to complete the transaction.

On a busy day (such as Mother's Day in North America), if a family is repeatedly blocked when attempting to call their grandmother, the family rightfully considers the switched service unusable, even if they can complete calls anywhere else in the world.

If the only circuits available are of such poor quality that grandmother's voice is unrecognizable, or if the connections established are repeatedly disconnected, the family rightfully considers the service unusable. The customers' level of frustration is very high and they may be prepared to demand compensation. The service provider needs to address these problems immediately.

In contrast, because low and moderate levels of call blocking, poor transmission, or call cutoffs usually can be overcome by quickly reestablishing the call, these moderate degradations usually do not prevent customers from completing their transactions. Customer frustration is lower and the service is not unusable.

Of course, the service provider should take any occurrences of moderately degraded performance seriously and should limit them with stringent long-term performance objectives. However, the urgency with which the provider addresses these degradations will depend on that provider's desire to meet their long-term objectives over shorter time periods.

It is the concept of "usability" that ITU and T1 have adopted in developing availability standards for switched services. Two more recommendations applying to unswitched frame and cell-based connections share the concept of usability

These six ITU and T1 documents develop two performance parameters: service availability (SA) and mean time between service outages (MTBSO).

Referring to the definitions developed previously, the item is the entire network (or set of networks) designed to provide the switched service between the two end users. The function is a combination of connection set-up, transfer of user information, and maintenance of the connection. Only if :

■   the switched connection can be completed with a reasonable reattempt algorithm,

■   the transmission quality is sufficient for useful communications,

■   the calls can be maintained for sufficient time to complete the transaction.

Is the communications service defined to be usable, in the up-state, and available. If any of the three criteria fails, the conclusion is that the network is not usable for the communications function, and therefore the service is in the down-state and unavailable.

The fraction of time during which the service is available between a pair of end points is called the SA. The average time between down-states is called the MTBSO.

The standards define exactly how poor performance must be to be officially classified as unusable. They clarify how the availability state can be quickly ascertained; and they provide information on how one can measure SA and MTBSO between standard network interfaces.

End-to-End Perspective

The item evaluated by the SA parameter is the network or set of networks providing service between a given pair of end points (an end point is either a standard customer-network interface or a standard network-network interface).

SA is the percentage of time a usable call can be established and maintained between that pair of end points. By setting SA worldwide objectives, the standards bodies have endeavored to support directly the needs of users.

Conventional ways of evaluating switched service availability include measures such as trunk availability, switch availability, access link availability, and blocking measured over large populations of customers and circuits.

Each of these provides some information about customer experience, but none of them track directly the reliability of end-to-end connections. One thousand blocked calls on a single access line is a much more significant event than 1000 blocked calls distributed evenly across the switch.

A network average of 99.95 percent availability measured and reported is a positive statement about performance, except for the one-in-a-thousand customer who experienced 50 percent blocking.

As illustrated in the Mother's Day scenario, concluding that the service as a whole is available is inappropriate when the customer's most important call cannot complete.

The end-point-to-end-point perspective of the standards focuses attention on these types of individual customer experiences.

Managing Availability from the Service Provider Perspective

In private conversations with the author, several service vendors have indicated that they are experimenting with evaluating their switched services using parameters similar to SA and MTBSO. However, to the author's knowledge, currently no service providers publicly describe their end-to-end performance in these terms.

There are at least two major concerns raised by the prospect of managing networks to achieve SA and MTBSO objectives. These concerns are not addressed by the standards, but will be discussed.

Measuring SA and MTBSO

The first and perhaps main concern is in being able to measure and monitor these complex performance parameters. Strictly speaking, in order to exactly evaluate SA and MTBSO, one would have to implement and track separate outage thresholds on blocking, transmission quality, and premature disconnects. This information would then need to be combined with information about access outages.

In reality, poor transmission quality and excessive premature disconnects need never contribute to service unavailability. Service providers can build their networks on principles that ensure these phenomena never exceed their outage thresholds.

Real-time monitors of transmission quality can detect severely degraded performance before the link becomes unusable (and/or before a PDS would be declared). The network should disconnect existing calls on this degraded link and then exclude it from use in subsequent calls until repairs are complete.

Other premature disconnects may be caused by other kinds of failing equipment. Network procedures should detect this failing equipment and eliminate it from service well before exceeding the premature disconnect threshold.

The net effect of these actions is to convert all severe transmission and disconnect problems into demand for new calls.

Alternative routing schemes then route these new calls, avoiding a repeat encounter with the same problems.

Thus, the switched network customer would never detect excessive transmission or disconnect problems and never attribute any unavailability to these types of problems.

When there is insufficient spare capacity to route around the problem, the new calls should be blocked and any unavailability will manifest itself as high blocking. A network service designed using these principles will be able to measure unavailability simply by monitoring short-term call blocking and access outages.

Why were transmission quality and premature disconnects included in the definition of unavailability? For the customer, there are no guarantees that the network was built using the above principles.

From the customer perspective, any aspect of the network design or operation that makes the service unusable is equally devastating. Defining the parameter using both the call set-up and the user information transfer parameters gives the customer equal recourse in the event the network is either working poorly or designed poorly.

Quoting Available Performance Objectives

A second concern relates to how the availability performance is described in terms meaningful to the customer. The definitions of SA and MTBSO apply strictly to end-point pairs, but an individual customer subscribing to a public service is interested in a description of reliability relevant to all of their calling. A purchaser of virtual private network service also is interest in the reliability of their entire network.

In the standards, the availability objectives are intended to apply to every end-point pair on the network. For a domesticated switched network, the ITU established a (very conservative) objective of 99.5 percent SA for all network end-point pairs. In other words, new customers to this service can be told that, at any time, they have at least a 99.5 percent probability of obtaining a usable connection to the party of their choice.

The level of performance that will be encountered during that connection will be governed by the service objectives for blocking, transmission, and cutoffs. On the other hand, up to 0.5 percent of the customer's attempts to communicate may encounter extremely degraded performance and be unusable.

Similarly, for a virtual private network customer, the probability of being able to complete a usable call on demand between any of their end-point pairs is at least 99.5 percent (again assuming conformance with the ITU). When the customer is interested in the network average availability, and the availability is known to differ among end-point pairs the average should be computed over all end-point pairs for which there exists traffic.

In other words, if there are n active end points all communicating with each other, then the network average is taken over n(n-1)/2 separate availability measurements. If there is never any expectation of communication between certain pairs of end points, these end-point pairs may be excluded from the average.

Weighting the average by the expected levels of traffic between end-point pairs can be useful as an estimate of the impact of unavailability on call volumes or revenue.

Finally, there is a concern that a single major facility or equipment outage may be sufficiently long by itself to cause the availability objective to be missed. The intuitive solution is to quote availability performance objectives only over long periods (e.g., one year). To be more responsive to customer needs, the availability performance may be quoted for shorter terms (e.g., three months).

Survivability and Service Availability

At this point we digress form a strict end-to-end focus to describe what network providers are doing to improve reliability. There has been much effort recently, particularly in the United States, to design robust networks and avoid service disrupting events.

Dynamic cross-connects and the architectures are being used to route around failures and to reallocate capacity during overload.

To evaluate network survivability, parameters are being developed that tie directly to maintaining high levels of switched service availability. The techniques for improving network survivability and the parameters for its evaluation are described in a draft T1 technical report.

The purpose of this digression is to relate the concepts of customer-oriented switched service availability to this important survivability work. Network outages and survivability are measured using a triple (intensity, duration, and extent) (I, D, E).

The intensity of the network outage is the depth of the problem as it manifests itself to the customer (e.g., percentage blocking, percentage of frame, packet or cell loss, or fraction SES). The D parameter of cell loss, or fraction SES). The D parameter of the (I, D, E) triple, quantifies the duration of the outage.

The E parameter quantifies the geographic area, population, or traffic volume affected by the outage. The three parameters can take on continuous values and define a three-space. Conceptually, the three-space divides into regions representing various network outage categories ranging from no outage to minor outage to major outage to catastrophic outage.

The Committee T1 terminology describing network outages is still being finalized, but it is clearly related to the concepts of service availability described earlier. The intensity parameter, I, can be easily associated with the customer-oriented availability threshold.

The duration parameter, D, can be associated with length of the minimal test for the availability state. The extent parameter, E, can be related to the number of end-point pairs affected by the network outage. If, for one or more end-point pairs, the I parameter is worse than its unavailability threshold for a period, D, longer than the minimal availability test, the network outage is creating service unavailability.

Network providers are considering measures of survivability based on the (I, D, E) triple. By choosing appropriate values for I and D, these providers will be monitoring availability as defined for end users.

By looking at various values for the number of end-point pairs, E, they will be bringing focus onto the needs of customers and user communities.

Summary

Public standards are defining availability and reliability for switched services based on a model of how the customer views the service. The resulting definitions quantify the total ability of a customer to place a call to a desired destination and complete a transaction. The standards include customer-oriented techniques for measuring availability.

Although the standards do not suggest techniques for maintaining switched service availability, this article includes some suggestions. In the face of ever-increasing customer expectations, this customer-oriented view of availability should serve as the basis for improving the future reliability of switched services.

Framework for Measuring Service Outages

The need for developing a methodology for quantifying service outages is clear. This need has been recognized by the FCC, the industry, and telecommunication users.

The scientific approach is to develop metrics, methodologies, and tools for quantifying characteristics of an outage. This will lead to a scientific assessment and control of various aspects of telecommunications service outages.

The preliminary definitions and notations necessary for developing a framework for measuring network outages are now developed.

The approach used here is based on an end-on-end customer perspective. In relation to the reliability of CSN, customers' concerns can be classified into three major questions:

1.   What is the chance that my existing communication path and/or my new communication establishment attempt fails (call cutoff and call establishment failure respectively)?
2.   For how long is the above condition going to continue?
3.   To how many and what destinations does this condition exist?

This has motivated the concept of triple components of a network outage initially introduced in April 1992.

Triple Components of an Outage

The customers' perspective of a network outage can be classified into three major components of intensity, duration, and extent defined as follows:

Intensity: The magnitude of force of a failure on a unit of usage. A unit of usage is the ability of establishing and/or maintaining a single communication from a source to a target. Intensity quantifies the impact of the outage on a unit of usage.

The higher the intensity of an outage, the lower the ability of communication. Let I denote the intensity of an outage.

Duration : The time period during which the outage, as defined previously, exists. Let D denote the duration of an outage.

Extent: A measure of the outage's spread. In general, it could consist of one or several characteristics such as the range of geographic areas and their population, type of application and service, time of day and/or year, and customers' communications pattern and volume. Let E denote the extent of an outage.

The (I, D, E) triple provides a framework for measuring network outages. The Committee T1-Telecommunication Working Group (T1A1.2WG) on the network survivability performance project has adopted the (I, D, E) triple framework (the only difference is that they use the notation terminology U, unservability, instead of I, intensity).

The framework can be applied to different networks and services. Each network and/or service needs its own specific formulae and computational procedures. Specific formulas are needed to express the I, D, and E in terms of characteristics and parameters of the corresponding networks and/or services.

Procedures and measurement systems must be specified and/or developed to estimate (approximate) corresponding characteristics and parameters leading to the quantification of I, D, and E. The next section demonstrates an application of the framework to the CSN.

The Reliability of LEC Telephone Networks

Many profound changes have occurred in global telephone networks in the last decade. The proportion of digital switches has increased dramatically. Optical fiber has become the transport medium of choice.

Common channel signaling (CCS) and signaling system No. 7 (SS7) have brought a whole new set of services into the networks. Despite these profound changes, local exchange carrier (LEC) networks are extremely reliable.

The purpose of this section is to describe that reliability using diverse sources of information.

Because LEC networks as more flexible and faster than ever before, and because they are more powerful, they are depended on more and more by millions of customers who have high expectations of their reliability.

The availability of network switches is at least 99.998 percent, meaning that 99.998 percent of the time a customer wants to make an interoffice call, the switch will be up. The paths between switches are also very reliable.

The chance that the path between two switches is available is 99.99 percent. Finally, for inter-office calls involving two switches, the availability of the interoffice network is estimated to be 99.99 percent.

Measuring Network Reliability

Network reliability is not a new topic. Over the last 15 years, there have been several attempts to measure the telecommunications network reliability. A major component of a measurement scheme is the collection of information when the network, or a portion of it, is in service.

Most data on network reliability consist of reported network outages or failures. This is logical, since most of the time the portion of the network that a customer can access is functioning correctly, and collecting information on the rare disruptions saves space and time.

A great deal of care is required to ensure that the data are complete and representative. If incomplete data are used indiscriminately, the result is overestimated network availability (up-time).

What constitutes a network outage is not as clear as it once was. Not all outages affect all services or all types of calls. For example, only call waiting may not be functioning for a period of time. As another example, an STP outage has no direct effect on intraswitch traffic.

There is no consensus regarding how long an outage should last to be counted in outage databases. Popular values include two minutes, 15 minutes, and 30 minutes.

The primary goal of collecting detailed reports on each of a few long outages is to reduce the number of outages of that duration, thereby improving the network. It is nearly impossible to set up teams to address every outage, so the number of outages that have detailed reports should be determined by the resources available to investigate the outages.

That is, if about ten outages per quarter can be investigated in detail, then the threshold should be chosen so that about ten outages are investigated. For this purpose, a large threshold of 30 minutes or longer would be appropriate.

Defining When the Network is Down

In devising ways to measure network reliability, we first note that most portions of LEC networks are up almost all the time. Defining when a portion of the network is down is more complicated than appears at first glance.

Should we count a portion of the network down if call waiting cannot be activated? Should we count a portion of the network down if no inter-LATA calls can be made? Should we count a portion of the network down if access to operator services is not possible? How many lines must be affected for an outage to be counted?

Even after we have decided which outages should be counted, we must decide how to measure network reliability. In this article, we measure network reliability in two ways: availability or, equivalently, up-time; and probability that a customer does not experience an outage longer than five minutes in a year.

Availability tells us the chance that a network is up when a user at a random time attempts to make a call. For example, if the availability is 99.998 percent, this means that 99.998 percent of the time the network is in service when a user attempts to make a call.

The second item above describes the chance that a customer will not see a five-minute-or-longer outage during an entire year. If this probability is 90 percent, then, on the average, a customer will not even see a five-minute outage for nine years out of ten.

Improving Network Reliability

Network reliability depends on three factors:

1. The reliability of individual components.
2. The repair process.
3. The architecture of the network.

By improving the reliability of each piece, equipment fails less often, and there is less chance for a network outage.

In LEC networks, the hardware failure rate of equipment has improved at least ten percent per year over the last ten years. The improvement is even more dramatic for highly complex equipment.

The architecture of LEC networks can add redundancy, which is present almost ubiquitously in the United States, at vulnerable spots. A network is designed in such a way that individual failures do not matter. At the fiber level, there are protection circuits. There are duplicated processors in end offices. Also, there are back-up power supplies in all end offices.

Congestion Controls in SS7 Signaling Networks

With the increasing penetration of common channel signaling (CCS) in telecommunications networks comes the attendant complexity of ensuring the integrity of the signaling network itself under conditions of stress.

In recent history, there have been some remarkable failures induced in public networks by failures of the CCS network, and where congestion controls (or lack of them) have played a significant role. These occurrences focus attention onto the importance of the correct operation of CCS congestion controls as signaling networks become larger.

Some Causes of Congestion

The signaling network management functions include not only congestion controls, but also the availability control procedures that reconfigure the network to allow traffic to avoid failed links and nodes.

These controls are not congestion controls per say, but their invocations represent the major cause of congestion in the signaling network, as traffic from failed network components is redirected to the remaining links and nodes. Congestion simply due to excess traffic is less likely because of the intentional over engineering of the signaling network links, although focused overloads of the signaling network are possible.

Before describing the congestion controls proper, we present a brief overview of network availability controls.

Link Changeover

Changeover is a signaling traffic management function for the diversion of traffic from a failed link to one or more other links.

It is a complex procedure designed to avoid message loss, duplication, or mis-sequencing.

The change-back procedure is then used to divert traffic back to the link when it becomes available again. Changeover is important to congestion controls because it presents a high transient load during the changeover to the link(s) that carries the diverted traffic.

Transfer Prohibited

Transfer prohibited (TFP) is used toward adjacent nodes for traffic diversion from unavailable nodes. The local route management function generates the TFP message for one or more adjacent nodes.

At nodes that receive the TFP messages, the local traffic management function exercises a forced rerouting procedure to route traffic away from the unavailable route. (No distinction is made between unavailable route and unavailable node).

When a route is again available, the transfer available (TFA) procedure is followed involving the transmission of TFA messages to adjacent nodes, where the local traffic management function may invoke a controlled rerouting procedure to reuse the now available route.

Transfer Restricted

Transfer restricted (TFR) is used toward one or more adjacent nodes for traffic diversion to alternative routes (if possible) in response to traffic congestion. The local route management function uses a TFR message to carry the indication to adjacent nodes.

At a node in receipt of a TFR message, the local traffic management procedure invokes a controlled rerouting procedure, in an alternative link set is available, to redirect traffic away from the congested route.

When a route is again available, the TFA procedure is followed involving the transmission of TFA messages to adjacent nodes, where the local traffic management function may invoke a controlled rerouting procedure to reuse the now-available route.

Comments

The possibility of coordination between the SS7 network congestion controls and the overload controls in the exchange call processing application is largely unexplored, but must be an issue of prominence given the possibly devastating nature of network failures due to CCS network congestion and failure.

The performance of the SS7 congestion controls cannot be properly considered in isolation.

For example, the discard of IAMs in the CCS network leads to reattempt in the call network and additional load on the CCS network.

Although the SS7 network congestion controls can be tuned to protect the signaling network, the overall impact on the call-carrying user network (e.g., PSTN, ISDN) should be considered.

Security Planning

Network Disturbances

In network planning, the network is appropriately dimensioned to carry a specified traffic load in its normal state. However, the network is sometimes disturbed by overload or system failures.

In order to maintain quality of service, the network should be designed to minimize the effects of disturbances. The characteristics of network disturbances will be analyzed before discussing countermeasures.

Overload

The network capacity is normally calculated to carry busy hour traffic. Some abnormal traffic overload may cause network congestion which may spread to the rest of the network.]

Public holidays may cause traffic overload, for example, which produces congestion. This overload is predictable. Railway accidents, snowstorms or radio station programs (such as those involving responses to contests) may cause localized overload which is unpredictable.

System Failures

The network consists of many elements such as switching systems, radio transmission systems, cable transmission systems, etc. When one part of one of these systems fails, the network capacity may decrease. The system failure can also produce network congestion due to a decrease of network capacity.

Counter Measures Against Disturbance

Overload

Network control and/or an increase in network capacity are possible countermeasures for disturbances due to overload.

Rerouting and traffic restriction are primary network controls. Rerouting control sends overflow traffic to a circuit group that is not in the normal route advance sequence, and is generally used when all normal routes are busy. Rerouting is a positive action, but it involves two problems:

1.   choice of the new route,
2.   and effect on circuit congestion.

On the other hand, while traffic restriction is a negative action, it is still a useful control action. These measures are generally discussed as network operations, coming under the general heading of network management.

In order to increase the network capacity, it is necessary to use all available duct space, exchange accommodation, etc., to the utmost, or to add redundancy to the network.

The former may be possible, if there is much accommodation available, but it causes many operational and maintenance problems. The latter may be useful, but may result in over-dimensioning problems.

System Failures

Various efficient countermeasures are possible concerning systems failures in the network. A network which is both highly reliable and economical would be realized by the optimum combination of various countermeasures.

The following measures are useful to prevent or minimize network disturbances due to system failures::

- Improvement in reliability of a network element;,
- reducing the failure rate for the equipment itself,
- improving the availability of the systems,
- provision of automatic changeover to standby systems, as used in microwave radio transmission systems,
- duplex configuration, as used in power supply systems,
- Improvement in reliability of the total network, by considering the network configuration,
- static security measures (furnishing an appropriate redundancy to the network and choosing an efficient network configuration),
- route diversity,
- double routing,
- load partition,
- dynamic security measures (supervising the network function and controlling the network,
- network security switching (network management).

Objectives and Scope of the Network Operating Plan

The principle objective of a network operating plan is to ensure that the elements of the network are used in an efficient and economic manner so as to ensure that the designed grade of service is achieved.

To meet such an objective an Administration must undertake certain operational processes, the most fundamental of which are maintenance, network administration, service provisioning and network management.

To a great extent the efficiency of these processes depends upon the availability and timeliness of "network surveillance data".

Thus, the subject of network surveillance is treated as an operational process in its own right. Each of these operational processes is defined at the beginning of the respective sections in this chapter, and is depicted diagrammaticaly in Figure 30.

Although the five operational processes mentioned above are treated separately in this chapter, it is important to remember that they mutually interact to pursue the overall objective of meeting the designed grade of service for the network.

The network operating plan must define the functions and responsibility of each of the required operational processes, and must specify how they are to be organized and implemented within the administration concerned.

The implementation of network operating plans continually evolves; the evolution matches that of the network and is equally complex. The manner in which the operational processes are provided in an Administration will depend on the level of development of its network.

All processes need not be provided in detail initially, particularly in less developed networks. Figure 31 provides an outline of a typical evolutionary approach to implementing operational processes.

It is important to consider investment costs for such recently introduced tools as minicomputers as a trade-off against the labor costs saved and the increased utilization of the network.

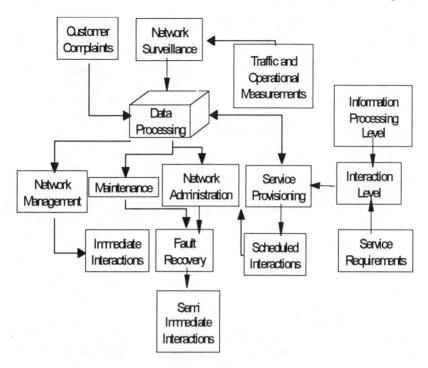

Figure 31:   Interactions between network operational processes

Maintenance

Background

The objective of the maintenance process is to ensure that installed network equipment operates in accordance with its specifications and subscriber services function as designed. Maintenance processes are concerned with the prompt detection, location, and repair of individual network elements.

These processes are triggered by referrals from network surveillance (which takes a global view of network service and performance problems), by subscriber service problems, by failure indications produced by specific network elements (both automatically and through routine testing or observation) and by referrals from network administration.

In modern networks, maintenance is undergoing revolutionary changes brought about by new concepts that effect the operating organizations, by the advent of remote surveillance and testing techniques, and by the use of computers in maintenance support systems.

These techniques and the new maintenance systems evolving from them pervade nearly every area of maintenance activity. New systems are available for maintenance of subscribers' lines, exchanges, circuits, transmission systems, and leased circuits. Many additional systems are under development.

Another area of major improvement in new maintenance support systems is that of mechanized records for all the transmission and switching equipment being monitored. This is an extremely important area.

Maintenance Approaches

Maintenance can be divided into the three broad categories:

1.   preventive maintenance,
2.   controlled maintenance, and
3.   corrective maintenance.

Preventive Maintenance includes routine procedures such as lubrication, cleaning and adjusting. It also includes detection of incipient faults before they affect service; this may be accomplished by routine and marginal testing procedures.

Controlled Maintenance is a form of preventive maintenance which, instead of being performed regularly, is applied when the frequency of faults indicates that preventive action is necessary.

Corrective Maintenance is based solely on fault finding after service has been affected. It involves a number of separate services:

Fault Detection: recognizing that a fault exists. Faults in subscribers' equipment and some faults in subscriber lines are usually detected by subscribers themselves. Faults in exchanges and transmission systems can usually be detected automatically and in most cases the offending circuit or equipment unit is automatically removed from service

Fault Notification : alerting maintenance personnel to the existence and severity of a fault. Once a fault has been detected and the associated information is available, maintenance personnel are notified so that they may begin corrective actions. The fault notification may have an audible alarm associated with it.

Fault Verification: determining if a reported fault still exists. A considerable time may elapse between fault notification and the start of fault location. Experience has shown that many fault indications transient and may or may not recur. First priority is given to correcting verified faults.

Fault Clearing: on-site action is required in some instances. In other cases, the defective unit can be removed and replaced with a spare via remote, manual or automatic control.

Service Verification: after the repair is completed, the maintenance person should verify that the fault has been cleared.

Service Provisioning

Introduction

The objective of the service provisioning process is to respond to service and circuit demands by arranging and connecting equipment and channels. Service and leased circuit demands are originated by subscribers and interexchange circuit demands are generated by the forecasting activities in the network administration process.

The service provisioning process can also be invoked indirectly by other events such as tariff revisions which may stimulate or suppress demand for service, or may require charging equipment installation or modification

Service orders are prepared in response to requests for service from subscribers. To provide service, it is necessary to select the subscriber line plans including cable and the cross-connections at flexibility points in outside plans, to select and connect exchange line and number equipment, and to install equipment at the subscriber's premises

Interexchange circuit orders may be initiated by traffic engineers or by the network administration process, if used. An interexchange circuit consists of all the elements between exchanges. This includes circuit relays, traffic usage registers, tie cables, test jacks, cross-connections on network frames and main frames, terminating and signaling equipment, and transmission channels.

When digital exchanges and PCM transmission are used, the variety of components in an interexchange circuit may be reduced due to the integration of signaling, transmission and switching.

Leased circuit orders are prepared in response to requests from subscribers for special services. Leased circuits can be voice or non-voice and include PABX circuits, out-of-area exchange lines, private lines, and circuits for private switched networks.

Elements include equipment at the subscriber's premises, local subscriber line assignments, terminating and signaling equipment as required, and channels in transmission systems.

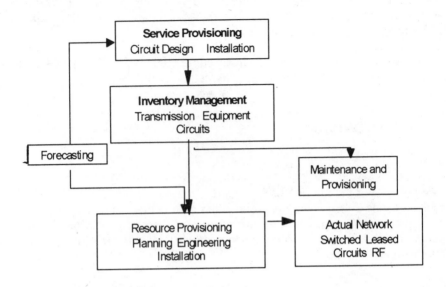

Figure 32: Inter-exchange and leased circuit provisioning

Network Surveillance

General

The purpose of the network surveillance process is to monitor the whole network, subscriber-to-subscriber, to ensure that proper grades of service and performance are maintained.

Network surveillance provides information for the personnel responsible for network administration, management, and maintenance, to permit efficient and accurate planning and operation of the telecommunications network.

Sources of Information

There are several sources of information which should be available to determine the quality of subscriber service and equipment performance which a network provides. These include a service evaluation system, either manual or automatic indicators of blockage, such as lamps actuated when all circuits are busy and, most important, data on the offered load, completed calls and circuit occupancy

Service Evaluation Systems

A summary of evaluations of each individual call and call attempt placed on a network would provide the most accurate measure of the quality of service. However, this would be very impractical and a very small though statistically correct sample should in practice be adequate.

Service evaluation systems automatically select individual call attempts to be evaluated, taking into account the particular quality to be sampled. Both the statistical nature of selection and the quality sampled may be manually determined.

The service evaluation procedure should observe the speed of response of network elements, network blockages, failures to complete, quality of transmission and any abnormalities. Service evaluations can be manual or automatic.

Fully automatic methods provide more accurate measurements and do not intrude upon the privacy of communications, but are less effective in determining transmission quality and abnormalities, as they do not have the benefit of user comments.

Data Acquisition

General

In a general sense all measurements, checks, fault reports, etc. are forms of data. They are transmitted in various ways to the relevant destinations and acted upon accordingly.

They may be in the form of handwritten messages, completed forms, alarm signals or encoded data. Use of the simpler data items in network planning has already been discussed.

Data Required

These can be listed as follows:

- details about the network (e.g., routing and signaling plan),
- fault reports,
- equipment performance,
- traffic measurements,
- billing/charging data.

When organized together, these form the basic operational statistics for the network.

Analysis of Data

In almost all cases, basic data must be analyzed and presented to make it suitable for two particular purposes. where information is required in real- or near-real time, some data (e.g., for network management) may need to be analyzed within an SPC exchange.

In this connection it may be noted that the processing ability of SPC exchanges varies with type and manufacture. In most cases, data will be processed by computers elsewhere so as to avoid inefficient use of the SPC processing capacity.

Finally, some data may require manual analysis.

Careful analysis of data can reveal many problems, and may thus be of great benefit in the prevention of serious failures. From the operational statistics or data collected and their subsequent analysis, the following reports can be made:

- fault reports, on different types of equipment, lines and transmission links,
- maintenance reports, on down times, fault clearing times, repair times and maintenance personnel occupation times,
- quality reports, on real transmission and switching performance and statistics which should include availability values,
- subscribers' complaints report,
- financial report, on used spare parts, personnel and loss of revenue.

Network Management

General

Manual telecommunications networks are protected against overload because the operator acts as a barrier between the customers and the network. With direct subscriber dialing, particularly of long distance and international calls, this barrier no longer exists and the control of input to the network is given directly to the customers.

Thus, networks which are engineered to handle a normal traffic load can quickly become overloaded when there is a large increase in customer calling.

This is particularly true of networks employing alternative routing and common control exchanges. The adverse effect of increased calling on network performance must be recognized, and means must be provided for network surveillance and control in order to ensure that the network performs in a highly efficient manner under the widest range of conditions that can be expected.

Benefits of Network Management

When the network is kept in an efficient and effective state by network management actions, significant benefits are derived by the customer and the Administration. Among the benefits are the following:

Impairments to customer service are dealt with on a day-by-day basis, particularly during unusual events. This can lead to:

- improved customer relations,
- stimulation of customer demand,
- increased revenue.

The network is used more efficiently. This can lead to:

- an improvement in the ratio of successful to unsuccessful calls,
- an increased return on the capital invested in the network.

There is greater awareness of the current status and performance of the network. This can lead to:

- a basis for establishing network management, maintenance, and restoration priorities,
- improved network planning information,
- improved information for deciding future capital investment in the network,
- protection of essential telecommunications, particularly during emergencies.

It is somewhat difficult to do a cost/benefit analysis for network management, since many of the above benefits are difficult to measure precisely. Cost/benefit evaluations of specific control actions are also difficult, since it is impossible to know what would have happened in the network if the control had or had not been taken.

Studies indicate that the improvement in network performance achieved by network management can be quite dramatic, with a rapid return of the capital invested in network management in some cases within one year.

It must be noted that network management does not replace the need to ensure that the network is adequately engineered to provide a satisfactory grade of service under normal load conditions: i.e., it does not replace network administration.

Optimization of the Physical Network

Statement of Problem

The aim of optimizing the physical network is to define the minimum physical layout cost of the transmission media consistent with satisfying a given demand for junctions between switching centers.

As previously mentioned, the physical network design has two aspects:

1.   the optimization of basic network structures including the layout of the transmission routes and the timetable for opening new routes. Most of the material below refers to this aspect of the physical network,

2.   dimensioning of the transmission routes, i.e., determining the number of pairs and/or transmission systems needed in a route or section to meet the junction demand, and when to install a new cable or system in an existing route.

Analysis of the Problem

The goals of physical network optimization are:

a.   to minimize the run length of any group of junctions interconnecting two switching centers,

b.   to maximize the number of junction groups which share the same path,

c.   to select for each connection the most economical transmission medium.

In many cases a) and b) are contradictory objectives. By satisfying a) the network cost is diminished, by reducing the length of the runs; but, on the other hand, savings based on economies of scale (the average cost per circuit is smaller as the total number of circuits in the group increase) are not obtained, as they could be by satisfying b). Finally, c) is interrelated with a) and b).

The dynamic aspect (the evolution of the physical network with time) cannot be disregarded. However, for a better understanding of the problem and its solution, a cross-sectional approach will first be studied.

An example, will serve to clarify these concepts. In solution a), the three exchanges are interconnected using the shortest path; in solution b) the connection between A and C follows the paths that connect A and B, and then B and C. In a) the total length of the junction circuits is smaller than that of b).

In b) the two network sections are each shared by two groups of junctions. Thus in these sections the cost per junction and per unit length is lower than in the same sections in a). The selection a) or b) will depend on the relative importance of the two cost factors (length of the junction circuits and economies of scale).

The selection of the transmission medium is the third factor, and is a function of the length of the route and the capacity required. Therefore, for both solutions the transmission medium selection should be studied, a process which will finally indicate whether solution a) or b) is to be preferred.

In considering the dynamic aspect of the design of the physical network, it is important to keep in mind that network evolution nearly always tends to require the opening of new routes, at least in those areas where the telephone density is far from saturation and there is continuously growing demand. However, in areas near saturation, and when introducing digital technology, planners must be aware that not all the present routes need necessarily be digitized or maintained in service.

In the example, it could happen that the more economical solution at a particular time would be b). However, if traffic between A and C grows, there comes a moment when opening a physical route from A to C would be justified.

Given the above, the appropriate method is to carry out cross-sectional studies for several dates (typically 2 or 3) during the planning period, in order to determine the optimum physical networks at those dates.

These networks are the basis for defining the growth in each of the network sections, and consequently for dimensioning the equipment to be installed in sections where extensions are required.

Resolution of the Problem

There is no commonly accepted method for optimizing the physical network. The optimization method described there has the characteristics of being relatively easy to apply and providing reasonably good solutions, although the optimum solution is not mathematically guaranteed.

The basic ideas of the method will be explained, assuming that the object is to design the physical network of a virgin area using only voice-frequency transmission facilities. Afterwards, the following points will be discussed:

- the influence of an existing network on the solution,
- selection of the transmission medium and network security implications.

For a better explanation of the problem see the following. If the need for circuits during the study period between points A and C cannot be met with the installed facilities, the planner can consider several alternatives::

- add a new cable between A and C,
- install a new transmission system or increase the capacity of the existing system,
- route the traffic by the route A-B-C, assuming that spare circuits exist in A-B and B-C.

The general problem deals with the following factors:

- selection of the most suitable transmission system,
- maximizing the use of existing plans,
- optimum timing and dimensioning for each section of the network, i.e., determination of the size of the extensions and when to make them.

The solution for a network as simple as the one in a) is not difficult, as the prelim is reduced to a simple economic comparison. However, to find the economically optimum solution in a large network is a laborious exercise
.
If the solution is to be obtained manually, the decision to use a given transmission system in any particular connection should be based on a point-to-point study. More sophisticated procedures can be implemented when computers are used.

Finally, when dimensioning the physical junction network, planners must take into account possible uses of the network other than for telephony, for example video, data, alarms, sound circuits, public clocks, connection of subscribers outside the service area, etc.

In some part of the town these services may occupy as many as 25% of the total circuits.

Functional Network

Statement of the Problem

The objective of optimizing the functional network is to find the minimum cost network able to provide a pre-established grade of service. As previously mentioned, to find the optimum network implies the determination of the structure of the network on the routing rules and the number of junctions between each pair of exchanges.

In general, finding the minimum cost network is equivalent to determining the network with the minimum equipment (i.e., junctures at exchanges and junctions between exchanges). This is only completely true when the cost of junctures and junctions is uniform throughout the network.

Since the amount of traffic to be carried by the network is predetermined, optimizing the functional network is equivalent to maximizing it efficiency, i.e., plans utilization.

Given the characteristics of the traffic and grade of service functions (see sections below), high efficiency in junctures and junctions is achieved by concentration of small packets of traffic.

Concentration implies the use of transit functions, which in turn implies duplication, triplication, etc., of the equipment involved in the establishment of a call.

To find an economically balanced position between these two factors (i.e., concentration for increased efficiency and decreased equipment, versus equipment duplication to achieve that concentration) is the objective of the optimization of the functional network.

The above statement refers basically to a cross-sectional approach. When time is considered, optimization seeks the minimum total cost for the whole planning period.

Analysis of the Problem

The basic items of input data for the optimization of functional junction networks are:

- Locations of the local exchanges and long-distance exchange(s) in the town.
- Traffic matrix corresponding to these exchanges.
- Grade of service.

- Costs.
- Constraints the present network state, exchanges' capabilities, etc.

The main factors for optimizing the functional network are:

- Efficiency of junctions.
- Traffic: amount and distribution.
- Service criteria: grade of service and transmission plan.
- Switching and transmission costs.
- Number and location of transit exchanges.
- Routing disciplines.
- Existing plans.
- Constraints on switching capabilities, security, etc.

Basic Network Configurations

Mesh Configuration

In this case all traffic is carried directly from the originating exchange to the terminating exchange. At the same time the individual routes of traffic A-B, A-C and A-D have their individual routes assigned and traffic does not mix.

When a call finds that all the circuits in its group are occupied, it is lost, regardless of whether the other occupied groups of junction circuits are congested or not.

Star Configuration

In this case all traffic passes via one transit exchange (T) (in other arrangements it may be through two transits in series).

All the traffic originated from exchange A shares the transit circuits between A and T, regardless of its destination. Similarly all the traffic terminated in one exchange shares the transit circuits that connect T with that exchange.

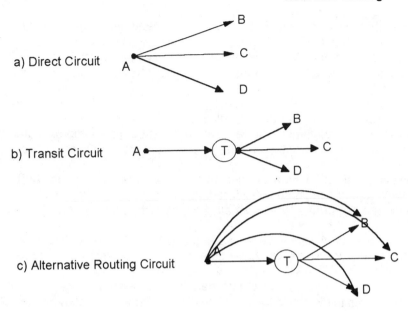

a) Direct Circuit

b) Transit Circuit

c) Alternative Routing Circuit

Figure 33: Direct, Transit, and Alternative Routing

Mixed Configuration

In this case mesh and star configurations are used simultaneously. For example, the traffic from A to B may be routed entirely by direct circuits and the traffic from A to C and D through the transit exchange.

Alternative Routing Configuration

This is a special mixed configuration using the capability of the switch try successively different ways to establish a connection. In the case of alternative routes, the switch first seeks the direct circuits connecting the originating and terminating exchanges and, if a free circuit cannot be found, the circuits between the originating and transit exchanges are sought.

The direct circuits are used by individual packets of traffic and, if traffic cannot find free direct circuits, the transit circuits are shared by the overflowing traffic.

There is an increase in costs of transit exchanges due to lower efficiency and to start-up costs associated with any new transit exchanges.

Although the transmission costs normally decrease, an increase of these costs in certain circumstances depends on the balance between shorter lengths of circuits and the need for more circuits (caused by lower efficiency and meaning that more terminal equipment is required when transmission systems are used).

The network cost is, in general, relatively insensitive to the number of transit exchanges. A relatively wide range in that number gives approximately equal costs if locations are optimum. In this sense the problem is not critical.

However, both the dynamic evolution of the network and the uncertainty of the demand forecast must be considered, if the solution is to be flexible (i.e., costs should not rise dramatically if small changes in the forecast occur).

For this aspect, it will be better in general to avoid the risk of having too many transits because some will have little use and the costs incurred will not be recovered.

It is easier and cheaper to create new transits and rearrange the routing of junctions than to dismantle transits. Thus the strategy to be followed here will be to keep the number of transits to a minimum.

Decisions about transit exchange locations cannot be separated from transit exchange numbers. When an additional transit exchange is considered, so must the area to be served by it be considered.

The only factor that affects the location of a transit exchange is the transmission cost of connecting it to the local exchanges in its area and to other local exchanges and/or transit depending on the chosen arrangement. In a local area, it is basically a problem of minimizing kilometers of wires and cables.

The location of transit exchange is normally not at all critical, so long as the distance between it and the source and main sink traffic zones is not large.

Routing Disciplines

The problem of selecting the routing discipline is that of selecting the transit through which passes each bundle of traffic (defined by an origin and a destination). Basically three rules are followed:

- routing through the transit in the area of the originating exchange,
- routing through the transit in the area of the terminating exchange,
- routing through both these transits in series.

The first rule will improve junction circuit efficiency and shorten circuit between originating and transit exchanges, but will cause longer and less efficient junction circuits in the connections between transit and terminating exchanges. Routing through the transits in the terminating exchange zones produces the opposite effects. For alternative routing, in practical cases, both rules give approximately equal results.

Other rules may be followed, such as routing through the transit that gives the shortest total length of both transit junctions circuits. The number of junction circuits will then be more than with the originating or terminating transit rules, and the circuit efficiency will decrease in general. This will be considered and evaluated in a discussion of exceptions which are sometimes economical.

In urban areas, junction networks generally present only one hierarchical level and consequently a maximum of only two transit exchanges are involved in a call. This is in contrast to long distance networks where two or three hierarchical levels are normally found.

To diminish the switching cost and to increase the flexibility, the combination of local and transit functions in the same switch is a practice being introduced with SPC systems, particularly with digital technology. This does not create any particular difficulty for junction network optimization.

Operational and security requirements favour a simpler routing scheme, to be adopted in preference to that which is theoretically the optimum, without incurring significant cost penalties. However, alternative routing planners must know that routing is more critical and requires more attention.

Constraints

The most common restrictions are caused by the switching equipment. In a local area the local exchanges have been installed at different times, using technology which at that time appeared perfectly adequate. In old equipment the lack of some of the capabilities of modern equipment sometimes imposes severe constraints on the junction network.

The most common, and significant restrictions are:

1.   A limitation in the number of outgoing routes.
2.   An inability to perform alternative routing.
3.   A signaling system in that some cases may prevent the establishment of some routes.
4.   Limitations in the number of incoming and outgoing junctures which the equipment can accommodate.
5.   A lack of full accessibility, or the parameters defining the accessibility when this is limited.

The first three limitations have imposed strong constraints in the past, particularly with step-by step switching systems. All, and in particular the first, have had more effect on the definition of network structures of many metropolitan areas than have any economic implications.

Other sets of restrictions arise from limitations on the extension of existing equipment, building space and location, etc. Finally, security requirements may influence the solutions chosen.

For example, protection against overloads may limit the efficiency of junction circuits, and protective measures against sabotage or disaster may influence the decision as to whether to split the transit function between two transits or to concentrate it on one.

Existing Plans

The main factors to be considered regarding existing plans are:

- Transit exchanges already installed.
- Transmission plans.
- Switching equipment and junctures at local exchanges.
- Capacity of buildings and their potential for extension.

The influence of the existing plans is greater when the network is being dimensioned and optimized in the short-term. Existing transit exchanges constitute a particularly strong constraint in the dimensioning/optimization of the junction network for the short-to-medium term.

Description of the Model

The main factors affecting the solution and their qualitative level of influence were discussed above.

The models that have been built mathematically to represent and solve (by computer) junction network problems generally follow the same basic ideas. They are differentiated mainly by detailed facilities included to accommodate peculiarities of particular networks.

Representation of Network Topology

In most models, network topology is represented by a matrix of distances between exchanges. These distances must, in general, correspond to actual lengths of the transmission media used between exchanges.

Traffic Demand

Traffic is represented by a matrix containing the traffic between any pair of exchanges. If, in the same building, different switching units use separate groups of junctions they are considered as different sinks/source for traffic. Long-distance traffic is also included.

Traffic Models

For offered (fresh) or pure random traffic, the Erlang B formula is normally used. Other formulas may be used, and models exist in which the planner can select which formula to apply. For second-choice traffic, given its peaky character, one parameter alone is not sufficient.

The general practice is to represent overflow traffic by two parameters, mean and variance, following Wilkinson's theory. Other formulas may also be applied.

Grade of Service

Models are normally based on one of the GOS criteria of final trunk group blocking or exchange-to-exchange blocking. In other models the user may select the criterion to be applied.

Costs

There are two main parameters that have to be considered. Fixed costs and Operational costs. Under Fixed costs we can include the costs of switching equipment, transmission etc. Under Operational costs are the monthly reccuring costs such as the cost of lines, leases etc.

<u>Switching equipment</u>

In the most general case the switching cost may be represented by:

$C = A + B \times$ No. of lines $+ D \times$ traffic in Erlangs $+ C_1 \times$ No. of junctures of class 1 $+ C_2 \times$ No. of junctures of class 2 + etc.

Admitted classes of junctures are analog with different signaling types, digital, unit- and bi-directional, etc.

Costs associated with the switch, such as power supply, building space, etc., will be included in the above formula. In general, the parameter associated with the number of lines is taken into account under the "Operational Costs".

Transmission Costs

All the discussion about transmission media cost is applicable here. In general, the models must include the different classes of transmission media applicable to the different types of junctures.

Network Structure and Routing

Models are generally only able to deal with one level of hierarchy, although other models may accommodate two or more levels. The routing disciplines used will be at least the terminating transit, the originating transit and the double transit. Other routing rules may also be able to be used.

In the approach given here both factors are considered as input data.

Other Considerations in the Model

Routing Restrictions:

These restrictions are normally limited to specification or forbidden routes. Some sophisticated models may also accept a limitation on the number of different junctions that can be accessed by a given traffic packet.

The impossibility of performing alternative routing (star-mesh trade-off) is normally given as an exceptional event, using a predetermined symbol

Transit Size:

Some models accept the possibility of limiting transit sizes. This can be especially useful when existing transits may be near their limits of expansion.

Juncture Group Size:

Upper and lower limits for the number of circuits in each group of junctures are normally accepted. Some models also accept minimum incremental limits, which is especially useful when studying junction circuit group expansion.

Bi-directional Circuits:

Some models accept the possibility of selecting bi-directional junctions if economically justified.

Implementation

Summary

The implementation of a network will commence as soon as a PCS license is awarded to a wireless operator. Prior to the license award, provisions are normally made to commence high level planning in anticipation of a license being issued.

This will allow the operators to prepare adequately and optimize their existing resources. Advance planning of the implementation will also enable the operators to identify most requirements in terms of personnel, equipment, budget and resources and hence allow the company to commence operations immediately after the issuing of the license.

Implementation Strategy

The implementation plan assumes cell coverage similar to existing cellular operators. Specifically, a gradual deployment starting with the major centers and expanding into smaller centers within a 5 year period. Of course the speed of deployment will depend on may factors such as:

1.   Frequency availability/clearance
2.   Co-Location availability
3.   Local access availability
4.   Real estate availability
5.   Equipment availability
6.   Capital availability

The metropolitan areas will be interconnected using most probably existing fiber optic facilities provided by alternate carriers. Digital infrastructure will be used wherever possible resorting to microwave based transmission systems wherever needed.

The implementation will also be dependent on a number of alternate suppliers who would provide the interconnection facilities as well as co-location presence.

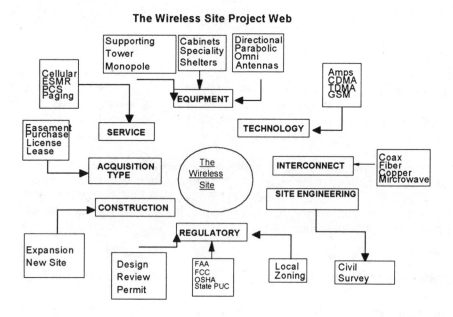

Figure 34: The Wireless Site Project Web

Five Year Implementation Plan

The 5 year implementation will depend on the subscriber growth hence capacity planning and required coverage. The coverage will gradually be expanded over a 5 year period to provide a coverage similar to the existing cellular operators.

The radio planning as well as the switching and transmission facilities will be designed in such a way so as to accommodate potential subscriber growths for a number of years to come.

PCS will be a highly competitive market and licensees will have incentives to construct facilities to meet the service demands in their licensed service areas. Nevertheless, minimum construction requirements may be necessary to ensure the PCS service is made available to as many communities as possible and that the spectrum is used effectively.

In some limited cases, some manufacturers may delay to supply the market with subscriber equipment opting to limit their resources for the much larger specific customer accounts.

The American PCS industry seems to agree that the first generation of PCS handsets will be dual-mode: either AMPS and DCS 1900 or AMPS and CDMA.

The rationale behind this equipment strategy is the fact that consumers rate ubiquitous coverage as the number one purchase influencer of wireless services. Given that the cellular industry took almost 10 years to deploy its current network, the most optimistic projections show that PCS providers will require 3 to 5 years to match the coverage of the cellular networks.

To minimize the coverage disadvantage of PCS providers, a dual-mode equipment strategy in conjunction with a cellular resale program will allow PCS providers to minimize their short-term disadvantages.

Of course the cost of dual-mode handsets may prove to be initially prohibitive for the majority of the consumers. In such a case, if operators still wish to use them for any reasons, they may end up heavily subsidising the cost of these handset.

Another factor driving North American service harmonization is the eventual development of North American partnerships and alliances between PCS providers in all three countries.

The ability to purchase equipment and services as a single entity, whether formal or informal, has obvious advantages. To share the learnings between the partners is another obvious advantage. But the most attractive advantage is the opportunity to use a single brand name and offer North American-wide seamless services.

14

Real Estate Acquisition

Summary

The following is a typical draft of a recommended plan and process review for acquiring sites for the operator's 2 GHz network.

One of the most important and immediate aspects of the operator's 2 GHz network deployment is the identification and acquisition of sites. The objective of this plan is to outline the recommended process and identify required resources. Commencing this work rapidly will enable a company to more quickly implement a 2 GHz network once the license has been awarded.

The Cellular and PCS Carriers

The A and B-side carriers have considerable financial resources and an existing cellular, microwave and probably a paging infrastructure. Therefore, their existing site inventory is a considerable asset which could be utilized for 2 GHz deployment.

Their co-location opportunities are far more extensive than the new PCS licensees currently. We should therefore assume that they have already completed the infrastructure design process.

The C-side carriers have only been awarded a license to operate recently, and as a result they will be entering the market with a delay. The process of site acquisition is a very important one and will determine whether an operator can have the complete or part of the network running.

Site Description

It is assumed that any PCS plan will assume similarities to today's cellular coverage.

There are three types of sites that will be required for deployment:

- Rooftop
- Tower
- Co-located (rooftop or tower)

Based on experience in the cellular industry as well as feedback from PCS carriers and vendors, some site types are preferable from a carrier's perspective. Rooftop sites are probably the most desirable due to the fact that zoning difficulties are drastically minimized.

Co-location, particularly for tower sites, should be pursued to minimize zoning difficulties, municipal push-back and construction costs. New tower builds should be avoided where possible as they will prove costly and may slow the deployment exercise due to zoning difficulties.

Microcells may also be a requirement for in-building environments.

Process

This section will discuss the steps involved in identifying, negotiating and securing a site.

Definition of Geographic Coverage

Marketing defines and prioritizes coverage on a city by city basis.   City boundaries must be established (by area code, CMA etc.) and in-service dates should be forecasted.

These in-service dates will be significantly impacted by regional spectrum clearance issues. They will also allow real estate to determine schedules and resources.

Municipal Zoning

This is probably the critical success factor within the site acquisition process. Zoning approval sometimes takes considerable time (2 to 6 months) in the cellular world. It is anticipated that zoning may prove to be even more difficult based on the increased volume of cellular, paging and microwave sites during the past five years.

There appears to be increased pushback from some municipalities, particularly for tower construction. Co-locating the operator's 2 GHz sites with existing cellular, paging and microwave sites may prove to be not only necessary, but common. Co-location will also reduce the aggregate acquisition and site construction costs.

Development of Coverage Grid (RF Engineering)

RF Engineering prepares a coverage grid for the city. This grid should provide the geographic coordinates for the ideal site locations. The grid will also provide the required number of sites for the coverage area which will allow real estate to determine resources.

Search Map Package Prepared

The single cell boundaries must be defined by street name (north, south, east and west). A larger scale map is prepared by real estate that marks the cell boundaries and the ideal site location, including geographic coordinates. The ideal height range for the site is communicated to real estate as well as the margin of flexibility (i.e., how far from the ideal coordinates can real estate search before the RF design integrity is jeopardized?).

Examination of Various Site Inventories

The operator's Real Estate department has normally significant relationships within the landlord community. An assessment can usually be made prior to the visual search of any buildings that may be available to the company through existing relationships and appropriate for 2 GHz purposes.

Other communications companies have numerous sites that may be required for co-location (cellular, microwave, paging, etc.). This information should be compiled immediately and mapped.

Then cross-reference these maps with the coverage grid designed by RF engineering. Potential sites are identified from these inventories and reviewed. These potential sites should be entered into a Site Management System (SMS).

Note:There is commercially available data software files by a number of companies that lists all sites in Canada that have been licensed by Industry Canada. The geographic coordinates for these sites (paging, microwave, cellular) are included along with a carrier identifier and a site name.

Area Search

Real estate, using the search map package, conducts a visual search of the area to identify potential site locations. Because there is no real estate data currently available (consistently) that includes geographic coordinates and municipal addresses, a hand-held GPS device may necessary.

Commencing the search as close to the ideal site coordinates as possible, the acquisition representative uses the GPS to measure the coordinates for the site alternatives. At the same time, the municipal address is recorded for future negotiation purposes.

These site alternatives are summarized for technical review.

Technical Review & Approval

There are numerous factors that have an impact on proper site selection and approval. Thorough review of these factors will ensure that short and long term operating expenses are minimized.

Some of the factors impacting proper site selection are:

■   Zoing and regulatory (variances, use permits, design reviews).

■   Interconnection (wired, radio/microwave).

■   Business (acquisition costs, estimated rents. access).

■   Engineering and construction (power, structural, environmental).

All of the above issues must be considered prior to commencing site negotiations. Please refer to the diagram below that summarizes the factors that impact a wireless site.

WIRELESS SITE IMPACT FACTORS

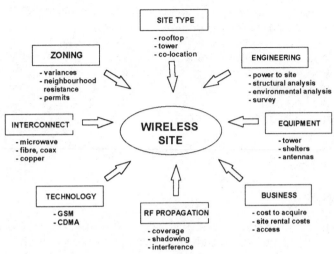

Figure 35: Wireless Site

Site Negotiation

Once the potential sites have been reviewed and approved, the negotiation process begins with the applicable landlords (contact, proposal, negotiation).

Real Estate can negotiate Options To Lease (tower sites, rooftop) and License Agreements (rooftop, co-location). Options typically include the general terms of the deal, such as rent amounts, term of the agreement, rights, etc.

Licenses can be structured such that the operator does not pay rent unless the equipment is installed.

Real Estate should negotiate with more than one potential site within each search area. This is done to protect the company in the event that one set of negotiations fails at any time.

 A lease or license can then be finalized with the site that is best for the company from both a coverage and a financial prespective.

All site negotiation status should be tracked in an Site Management System.

Permits and Approvals

A number of permits, approvals and documents are required before a site can be built. Some of required documentation includes:

- Site lease/license agreement.
- Landlord authorization and permission form.
- Survey (if required).
- Entrance permit.
- Industry Canada/FCC licenses.

Once the above documentation has been secured, the site can be released to the construction group for build.

Administration:

Once a site has been secured and released to construction for building, the administration process begins. A Subsriber Management System (SMS) should be utilized for document management and reporting.

Financial information can also be recorded in the SMS including rental payments, facilities costs, license costs, etc. Site termination's, renewals and changes must all be administered through an SMS.

Please refer to Figure 36 for a summary of the above process.

2 Ghz Site Acquisition: Process Flo

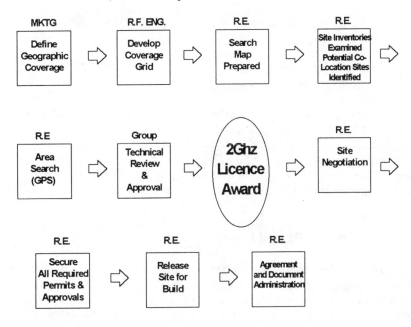

Figure 36: Site Acquisition Project Flow

Estimated Costs & Budget

The following will outline estimated costs that would be incurred during the site acquisition process.

Typical Site Rents

The site rental costs will vary depending on the type of area and the type of installation. It will also vary depending on the demand of the site. Certain sites happen to be at strategic locations in terms of RF planning. These locations will attract a high level of rental fees.

It is not unusual for landlords who own high visibility sites to request bids from a number of different operators so as to drive the site rental fee as high as possible.

Site Type	Estimated Rents
Rural or Corridor Site $1200 to $3600 per yr.	$100 to $300 per mth;
Urban Fringe Site $3000 to $6000 per yr.	$250 to $500 per mth;
Urban Downtown & Tourist $4800 to $12000 per yr.	$400 to $1000 per mth;

For budget purposes, an average of $1200 per month is assumed. 5% per year inflation is typically added to the rent amounts. The amounts above do not include any unusual high visibility sites which may demand unusually high rental fees.

Acquisition and Permit Costs

An exercise was conducted to determine acquisition costs assuming that the operator conducts all of the work in-house. Based on this analysis and experience in the cellular industry, it is estimated that it will cost approximately $10,000 to acquire a site and secure certain permits. The assumptions for this exercise are listed below.

Labor ($4320)

Calculations are for the acquisition of one site
Internal employee rate of $40 per hour
Total man-hours to hand-off available sites to construction are ..(to be Calculated by the planners).

Documentation/Permits ($4500)

Property survey and site plan is $3000
Municipal permits are $1500

Legal Costs ($300)

Assume average of 1.5 hours of review by our counsel at $200 per hour for each agreement.

Expenses ($436)

Transportation is $120 per site for mileage (@ $0.31/km)
Landlord meal/entertainment is $100 per site
Cellular air-time costs for reps is $216 per site (based on $300 per month bill).

<u>Administration ($150) plus Insurance</u>

Administration and handling of the documents (registration, signatures, entry
to SiMS, etc.) assumed to be 6 hours at $25 per hour ($150).

Steps/Status:

1. Site Acquisition Process Diagram.
2. Impact Factors on Wireless Site Diagram.
3. National Rollout Site Acquisition and Rent Budgets.
4. Maps.
5. Current inventories (cellular, paging, micro).
6. The operator's 2 GHz grid (will be produced through MCAP or similar package).
7. National Sites File (includes site name, carrier, coordinates).
8. Support for Co-Location.

15

Civil Engineering

Introduction

Civil Engineering contains the work that has to be put in place to built a network from a construction prospective.

Installation/Construction Standards

- Develop in house or contract out could produce a complete set of Civil/installation specifications in a few months.
- To develop the standards we will need some input from RF Eng.
- Type of antennas, lines, base station equipment, etc.
- Size of shelters will be defined.
- Height of towers/structures will be necessary.
- Microwave transmission? (towers designed for microwave antennas are much more expensive/limited).
- Use a partner (if applicable) as resource for specs.
- How often will the operator co-locate with competitors.
- Documentation group to administer the standards the operator compiles (drawings, as builds).

Standard Construction Contract

- Where to draw the line at legal construction practices, 25k, 50k (legal tendering, holdbacks, proper inspections, statutory declarations, etc.,) this can be very costly.
- Will the company tender its own projects, options.
- Turnkey to contractors (still require company construction staff).
- Use consultants to run construction.
- Employ project management firms .

Approved Contractor Policies

- Have to develop contractor/the operator's interaction policies.
- Standard commissioning procedures.
- Site access.
- Contacts for landlord issues.
- Scheduling policies/standards.
- Who will project manage the installations, the company or other?
- To what extent will contractors maintain the installations, operations staff?

Standard Floor Plans:

- What will the equipment look like, dimensions, number of pieces/racks?
- Will most sites be city/leasehold (leaseholds are difficult to standardize due to the odd shapes)?
- What businesses will we be in, how much growth space to leave?

HVAC Standards:

- Should be part of the standards package?
- What kind of loads will the equipment generate?
- Local manufacturers?
- Single supplier for Country/State (easier maintenance).

Container Standards:

- Security/vandalism.
- Rural or rooftop.
- Tower sites need ice protection.
- Power requirements of equipment.
- Backup power, gensets, batteries(loading).

Building Permits:

- Who will be responsible for obtaining, same for zoning, etc., or different groups?
- At what stage to apply, delays?
- Consider the expense.

Tower Approvals:

- Hostile Municipalities.
- Monopoles/aesthetic towers.

Towers:

- Aesthetic.
- Heights.
- Rooftop structures.
- Maintenance program.
- Consultants.

Towers and Masts:

- Monopoles.
- Guyed Masts.
- Towers.
- Soil Tests.
- Other Users.
- Antenna Platforms.
- Tower Design.
- Security.
- Tower, Mast and Monopole Maintenance.
- Repair.
- Tower Inspection checklist.

Cell Sites:

- How many, how fast?
- What types (rooftop, industrial, rural)?

Equipment Shelters

Switch Building

- Equipment Room, Control Room, Battery and Power Room.
- Emergency Plant Room, Roofing, Insulation Cladding, Floor Loading and Construction.
- Uncrating Area, Storeroom, Walls, Ceilings, Windows, Appearance, Internal Finishes.

Also,

- External Finishes.
- External Supply.
- Electrical Power Outlets.
- External Emergency Plant.
- Air-Conditioning.
- Typical Switch Room.

Base-Station Housing:

- Floor Loading.
- Additional Area Required?
- Weight, Lighting, Security, Equipment Mounting, Insulation, Cable. Window, Electrical, Access.

Grounds and Paths

Switch Centers:

The following are some typical questions asked by a company's project staff.

- How much company involvement, turnkey by contractors or switch supplier?
- Sizing, what businesses will the company be involved in into the future, how much space should be set aside for these future needs?
- How many switches will we need?
- Timing, switches will take 6-12 months to install.

16

Glossary and Standards

PCS Standards

Below is a slightly edited reprint of descriptions by TIA and ATIS of the seven proposed PCS air interface standards, beginning with the four that are furthest along (and offer full mobility) in the standards-approval process.

References to "licensed-band applications" apply predominantly to wireless networks that offer commercial service to subscribers. "Unlicensed bands" are for self-contained PCS products and services that operate similar to low-power cordless telephones. Time slots are used in Time Division Multiple Access technology to increase capacity.

Composite CDMA/TDMA

This is a composite Code Division Multiple Access/TDMA-Time Division Duplex air interface for a large-cell, licensed-band applications and a small cell, unlicensed-band applications. CDMA is used between cells and TDMA within cells. The proposal is based on technology developed by Omnipoint Corp.

DCS-based TDMA

This is an eight time-slot TDMA air interface suitable for high- and low-mobility and for large and small-cell, licensed-band applications. A derivative of Digital Cellular System 1800, the frequency-shifted variant of the Global System for Mobile communications 900 MHz air interface MCI Communications Corp., is working on this proposed standard.

Interim Standard-54-based TDMA

This is a three time-slot TDMA air interface for high- and low-mobility, licensed-band applications, capable of handling various cell sizes. Extendible to six-time slot TDMA with half-rate speech coders. Also, it is a derivative of TIA

IS-54 technology from 800 MHz cellular. Ericsson GE Communications Inc. is behind this proposed standard.

IS-95-based CDMA

This is a 1.25 MHz spread spectrum CDMA air interface for the PCS spectrum, suitable for high- and low-mobility, licensed-band applications, handling various cell sizes. It is a derivative of the TIA IS-95 CDMA technology from 800 MHz cellular, supports soft handoffs, uses variable-rate speech coders for capacity and supports a 13.3 kilobit per second user information rate. Qualcomm Inc. supports this technology.

The other three proposed PCS air interfaces expected to go to ballot early next year are:

PACS TDMA

The Personal Access Communications System proposal covers licensed and unlicensed band operations. For the licensed band, the specification is derived from the Wireless Access Communications standard by Bell Communications Research Inc.

There are two annexes for the unlicensed band, one based on the Japanese Personal Handy Phone System and the other on a derivative of the WACS.

It is an eight time-slot TDMA air interface with a Frequency Division Duplex (FDD) mode for small-cell, licensed-band applications and a Time Division Duplex (TDD) mode for small-cell, unlicensed-band applications. Motorola Inc. is pushing this technology internationally.

DCT-based TDMA

This is a 12 time-slot TDMA air interface for small-cell applications derived from the Digital European Cordless Telephone Standard. Work on a proposal for operation in the unlicensed band is being undertaken through a cooperative effort with another TIA Engineering Committee. This is another Ericsson-GE project.

Wideband CDMA

This is a 5 MHz CDMA air interface for large- and small-cell, licensed-band applications. The basis of this proposal is derived from wideband technologies supporting the aggregation of traffic channels within a radio frequency channel to support higher data rates.

Oki Telecom and InterDigital Communications Corp. are the masterminds of this approach

Network Service Quality

The judge of the quality of a telephone connection is the customer. A fundamental objective of transmission system planning is to ensure that the telephone customer will experience a perceived acceptable quality of performance, irrespective of the connection length or the transmission facility employed.

This quality of service is normally specified in terms of Grade-of-service.

Grade-of-Service

In North America, GOS is currently defined in terms of the distribution of customer subjective ratings of the quality of a particular telephone connection on a scale of excellent, good, fair, poor, and unsatisfactory.

The GOS is dependent on the characteristics of the circuit components from customer to customer including the acoustic-to-acoustic coupling characteristics of the telephone set.

The circuit performance characteristics that have been examined (mainly by the Bell System in the United States) are loss, noise, level, delay, and echo.

Echo

The major source of echo generation in the telephone network is the 2W to 4W hybrid interface. The reflected echo level is a function of the mismatch between the hybrid balance network Z_1 and the impedance Z_2 of the 2W path as seen from the hybrid.

The amount of annoyance caused by talker echo is a function of echo amplitude and the overall round trip delay.

In general, as the delay is increased the echo amplitude must be reduced to maintain the same GOS.

JTC Standards

The Joint Technical Committee (JTC) in the United States has been developing PCS technical standards for the past two years. The mission of the JTC is to develop standards and technical reports relating to user access to telecommunications networks through interfaces associated with wireless services and PCS. Both the wireless industry and regulatory bodies have recognized the JTC as leading standards body for PCS.

All the major wireless equipment manufacturers submitted PCS standard proposals with AT&T and Motorola submitting two proposals each and Ericsson submitting three proposals. Other standard proposals were submitted by Alcatel, Hughes Network Systems, InterDigital, Northern Telecom, Oki, Omnipoint, Panasonic, PCSI, Qualcomm and Siemens Stromberg-Carlson. Most of the vendors supported multiple proposals. The JTC's role was to evaluate the proposals.

The 17 proposals originally submitted by various manufacturers have been consolidated into seven key PCS air interface standards. According to Mel Woinsky, chairman of the T1P1 technical subcommittee, "Despite the large number, multiple standards for the diverse PCS industry is a logical move.

There are seven proposals because service providers are a diverse group and they may need or require a different technological approach to the market. The market, the service provider, will have an infrastructure technology choice, and its subscribers will determine the market,"

While having so many incompatible air interface standards raises network and handset interoperability questions, the JTC believes handset interoperability problems will be ironed out by the manufacturers.

The standards the JTC established include:

DCS-based TDMA is an 8-time slot TDMA air interface with licensed band application for high- and low-mobility using large and small cells. It supports multiple code as many as 16.

IS-54-based TDMA is a 3-time slot TDMA air interface for high- and low-mobility, licensed-band applications and is capable of handling various cell sizes. It is extendible to 6-time slot TDMA with half-rate speech coders; and is a derivative of T1A IS-54 technology from 800 MHz cellular.

IS-95 CDMA is a 1.25 MHz spread spectrum air interface, suitable for high- and low-mobility, licensed-band applications for various cell sizes. It was derived from 800 MHz cellular technology. It uses variable-rate speech coders, and supports a 13.3 Kbps user information.

Wideband CDMA is a 5 MHz CDMA air interface for large- and small-cell, licensed-band applications. It is derived from wideband technologies supporting the aggregation of traffic channels within a radio frequency (RF) channel to support higher data rates.

PACS TDMA is the personal access communications system (PACS) proposal; derived from wireless access communications system (WACS) from BellCore and the Japanese personal handyphone system (PHS). It has licensed and unlicensed band applications; is an 8-time slot TDMA air interface and uses TDD for unlicensed.

DCT-Based TDMA is a 12-time slot TDMA air interface for small-cell applications, which is derived from the digital European cordless telephone standard.   Work on a proposal for operation in the unlicensed band is being undertaken.

Composite CDMA/TDMA is a composite code division multiple access (CDMA)/TDMA TDD air interface for large-cell applications, using CDMA between cells and TDMA within cells.   It has licensed and unlicensed band applications, it is based on technology that received a pioneer's preference from the FCC.

Appendix

FCC Exhibit 13 - US/CANADA INTERIM SHARING ARRANGEMENT FOR 2 GHz BROADBAND PCS

PUBLIC NOTICE
FEDERAL COMMUNICATIONS COMMISSION
1919 M STREET, N.W.
WASHINGTON, DC 20554

DA 94-1 289
New media information •+1 (202) 418-0500. Recorded listing of releases and texts •+1 (202) 632-0002. Internet Anonymous FTP site: ftp.fcc.gov.

November 21, 1994

**US/CANADA INTERIM SHARING ARRANGEMENT
FOR 2 GHz BROADBAND PCS**

On November 14, 1994, representatives of the FCC and Industry Canada concluded a sharing arrangement for 2 GHz Broadband Personal Communications Services (PCS). This interim sharing arrangement provides for use of the 1850 to 1990 MHz band for PCS along the United States and Canada border. This sharing arrangement should assist parties intending to participate in the FCC auction process and should facilitate the eventual provision of PCS services along the border.

The principal provisions of this interim sharing arrangement are:

- The frequency band 1850-1990 MHz is to be shared on an equal basis and both countries are to have full use of these frequencies for the provision of PCS services.

- Additional use of the 1850-1990 MHz frequency band for fixed point-to-point microwave use is to be limited and discouraged and any new use of the 1910-1930 MHz band for fixed microwave operations is to be avoided. (The 1910-1930 MHz portion of the 1850-1990 MHz band has been designated for unlicensed PCS use in the United States and a similar type of use in Canada).

- Any new PCS use of these frequencies is not to cause harmful interference to existing fixed point-to-point microwave operations in the other country.

■   Coordination of all PCS systems within 120 km (75 miles of the border is required and will be based on: A technical analysis, using recognized industry procedures such as TIA/ELA Bulletin (TSBI0-F), that interference is not caused to existing microwave operations; or, alternatively,

i.   A mutually acceptable arrangement between the PCS and fixed microwave operators.

■   Licenses for PCS base station facilities within 72 km (45 miles) of the border will be conditioned to indicate that future coordination is required between PCS operators in both countries to ensure that interference is not caused to PCS operations in the other country and that the band is shared on an equal basis. (This is similar to actions taken during the initial licensing of the cellular radio service.)

■   The predicted or measured median field strength of any PCS base station is not to exceed 47 dBuV/m at any location at or beyond the border unless the affected PCS operators in the adjacent areas agree.

■   Compatible PCS operations at the border are best assured through coordination of operating and technical parameters by PCS operators; and, PCS operators are to notify the FCC and Industry Canada of any agreements. Such agreements are subject to review by the Agencies.

The full text of the arrangement has been placed in GEN Docket No. 90-314 and copies are available from international Transcription Service at (202) 857-3800. For further information, contact the Office of Engineering and Technology at (202) 653-8114 or the International Bureau at (202) 254-3394.

The attached document is an interim sharing Arrangement concerning the use of the 1850 to 1990 MHz band for Personal Communication Services (PCS) along the United States and Canada border, as agreed between representatives of Industry Canada and the Federal Communications Commission (FCC) during the Radio Technical Liaison Committee (RTLC) meeting held November 14, 1994.

**Interim Sharing Arrangement Between Industry Canada
and the Federal Communications Commission
Concerning the Use of the Band
1850 to 1990 MHz**

1.   Scope

1.1   This interim Arrangement between Industry Canada and the Federal Communications Commission, hereinafter referred to as the Administrations, covers the use of the frequency band 1850 to 1990 MHz along the Canada/United States border.

1.2   This interim Arrangement is subject to review at any time at the request of either Administration.

1.3   This interim Arrangement will be applied provisionally until the definitive entering into force of a replacement for the Agreement Concerning the Coordination and Use of Radio Frequencies Above Thirty Megacycles per Second, with Annex, as amended.[1]

2.   PCS Use of the Band

2.1   Both Administrations agree that the 1850-1900 MHz frequency band shall be shared on an equal basis along the border and that to the extent possible both Administrations shall have full use of those frequencies or sub-bands identified for the provision of Personal Communication Services (PCS) or similar type services within their respective countries.

3.   Existing Microwave Use of the Band

3.1   Both Administrations agree that additional use of the 1850-1990 MHz band for fixed point-to-point operations shall be limited and discouraged to the extent possible starting with the effective date of this Arrangement.

---

[1]Exchange of notes at Ottawa, October 24, 1962. Entered into force October 24, 1962. see USA: Treaties and Other International Acts Series TIAS 5205. CAN: Canada Treaty Series (CTS) 1962 No. 15. Agreement Revising the technical annex to the Agreement of October 24, 1962 (TIAS 5205/CTS 1962 No. 15). Effected by exchange of notes at Ottawa, Canada, June 16 and 24, 1965. Entered into force June 24, 1965. USA: TIAS 5833/CAN: CTS 1962 No. 15, as amended June 24, 1965.

3.2   Both Administrations agree that any new use of 1910-1930 MHz (which has been designated for unlicensed PCSS use in the United States and license-exempt PCS use in Canada) for fixed point-to-point shall be avoided after the effective date of this Arrangement.

4.   Coordination with Fixed Microwave

4.1   Both Administrations agree that the provision of any new PCS or other similar type services shall be on the basis that harmful interference is not caused to existing fixed point-to-point operations authorized by the other Administration.

4.2   Both Administrations agree to require coordination of all PCS systems located within 120 km (75) miles of the border. Such coordination shall be based on:

■   A technical analysis that interference is not cause to existing microwave operations of the other Administration. The analysis shall be based on recognized industry procedures such as, TIA/EIA Telecommunications Systems Bulletin (TSB10-F), "Interference Criteria for Microwave Systems;"

or

■   Alternatively, a mutually acceptable arrangement between the applicant/operator of the PCS facility and any affected fixed microwave operations.

4.3   In the event that there is interference from any PCS operation located beyond 120 km (75 miles) from the border, both Administrations agree to take appropriate steps to resolve such interference.

5.   Coordination between Licensed PCS Operations

5.1   Both Administrations agree that the following or a similar clause should appear on all authorization documents for PCS base station facilities within 72 km (45 miles) of the border:

"This authorization is subject to the condition that, in the event that systems using the same frequencies as granted herein are authorized in an adjacent foreign territory (Canada/United States), future coordination of any base station transmitters within 72 km (45 miles) of the Unites States/Canada border shall be required to eliminate any harmful interference to operations in the adjacent foreign territory and to ensure continuance of equal access to the frequencies by both countries."

5.2   Both Administrations agree that the predicted or measure median field strength of any PCS base station shall not exceed 74 dBuV/m at any location at or beyond the United States/Canada border unless the affected PCS operators in adjacent areas agree to a higher value and the Administrations agree.

5.3   Both Administrations agree that compatible independent operation of PCS systems on either side of the border will be best assured through coordination of pertinent systems operating and technical parameters by the PCS system operators. PCS systems operators shall carry out such coordination and the FCC and Industry Canada shall be notified of any arrangements agreed to, or in the event that a satisfactory arrangement is not reached. In any case, the arrangements reached by the operators will be subject to review by the Administrations.

References

Mazda, Fraidoon (1993), Network Management, Telecommunications Digital Network Design", Telecom Canada

"Telecommunications Engineers Reference Book" , Edited by Fraidon Mazda, 1993

"Information Document for Personal Communications Services", AT&T Network Systems, Release 1, November 1994.

"Networks and Telecommunications - Design and Operation" , Martin P. Clark,

"Trunk Traffic Engineering Concepts and Applications", Bell Communications Research Special Report SR-TAP-000191

"Digital Network Notes" - Telecom Canada

"Mobile Cellular Telecommunications" William C. Y. Lee, 1989

Bell Canada General Tariff (CRTC 6716)

Bell Canada Special Facilities Tariff (CRTC 7396)

Bell Canada Access Services Tariff for Interconnection with Interexchange Carriers (IXC's) (CRTC7516)

Stentor National Services Tariff (CRTC 7400-E)

CRTC Telecom Decision 94-19

Competition and Interconnection: The Case of PCS (July 1994)

K. C. Glossbrenner, "Availability and Reliability of Switched Services" IEEE Communications Magazine, Special issue on Dependability of Network Services, June 1993.

RCR, Industry begins voting process to pick nation's PCS standards Economies of PCS, Qualcomm.

M. Daneshmand and C. Savolaine, "Measuring Outages in Telecommunications Switched Networks" IEEE Communications Magazine, Special issue on Dependability of Network Services, June 1993.

Index

ABOUT THE AUTHOR

John Tsakalakis is a senior architect with IBM's
Telecommunications and Media Industry Solutions Unit
(ISU) in Toronto, Canada. Previous to IBM, he has held a
number of senior engineering management positions related
to the design and deployment of both wireless and wireline
networks in North America and Europe. He spearheaded
the design and deployment of PCS, and has presented in
numerous conferences as well as acting as a wireless consul-
tant to NORTEL among others.